The
Social Styles
Handbook

Adapt Your Style to Win Trust

Also available from Nova Vista Publishing:

Business Books
Win-Win Selling
Vendre gagnant-gagnant (French edition of Win-Win Selling)
Versatile Selling
S'adapter à mieux vendre (French edition of Versatile Selling)
Social Styles Handbook
I Just Love My Job!
Taking Charge of Your Career Workbook
Grown-Up Leadership
Grown-Up Leadership Workbook
Time Out for Leaders
Time Out for Salespeople
Get-Real Selling
Leading Innovation
Service Excellence @ Novell
What Makes Silicon Valley Tick?
Nature Books
Return of the Wolf
The Whitetail Fieldbook
Music Books
Let Your Music Soar

© 2004, 2011 Nova Vista Publishing

How to order: single copies may be ordered online at www.novavistapub.com. In North America, you may phone 1-503-548-7597. Elsewhere, dial +32-14-21-11-21.

ISBN 978-90-77256-33-6

D/2011/9797/3

Printed in the United States of America

20 19 18 17 16 15 14 13 12 11 10 9 8 7 6 5 4 3

Cover design: Wouter Geukens
Text design: Layout Sticker

Contents

Foreword by Larry Wilson 7

SECTION 1: THE CASE FOR COMMUNICATION 9

1. **Introduction** 9
   Words Aren't the Key 10
   Social Styles, Versatility and Success 12
   Summary 14

2. **Mindset Matters** 15
   A Warm-Up Exercise 15
      The Exercise 15
      The Point of the Exercise 16
   Essential Mindsets 17
      Mindset #1: Look for the Signals and Respond Correctly 17
      Mindset #2: Be Prepared to Act in Ways that Don't Feel
         Comfortable 17
      Mindset #3: You Can't Change Your Own Style,
         But You Can Adapt Your Behavior 19
      Mindset #4: Diversity is Enriching,
         But Requires Understanding 19
   Summary 20

SECTION 2: DIMENSIONS OF SOCIAL STYLES 21

3. **A New View of Behavior** 21
   Two Critical Assumptions 22
      Social Styles Focuses Only on Observable Behavior 22
      Perception is Reality 22
   Summary 23

4. **Assertiveness and Responsiveness –
   The Measures of Behavior** 24
   Assertiveness and Responsiveness 24
      Assertiveness – The Measure of Influencing 25
      Responsiveness – The Measure of Expressing 26
      Assertiveness and Responsiveness –
         The Basis for the Social Styles Matrix 28
   Summary 31

5. **Versatility – Adapting Your Style** 33
   Versatility in Action 34
   Comfort Zones – Yours and Theirs 34
   Summary 35

6. **Task and Relationship Tension –
   Productive or Unproductive?** 36
   Task Tension 36

Relationship Tension 37
Rising and Falling Tension 38
Moving from Relationship to Task Tension 40
Summary 41

7. **Comfort – The Key to Trust and Confidence** 42
Comfort Opens the Way to Trust 42
The Effects of Discomfort 43
The Payoffs for Making Others Comfortable 44
The Requirements for Comfort 46
Summary 47

8. **Habit – Getting Beyond Comfort and Custom
in Communication** 48
Comfort Zones and Habits 48
Adapting – Better than Just Reacting 50
Style Modification 51
Summary 53

9. **Generalizing and Judging – Pros and Cons** 54
When Generalization and Judgments Make Sense 55
Behavior, Feeling, and Thinking 56
Summary 58

10. **Back-Up Behavior – Fight or Flight** 59
Fight or Flight Tendencies 59
Back-Up Recovery Strategies – LSCPA 62
    Listen 62
    Share 63
    Clarify 63
    Problem-Solve 64
    Ask for Action 64
Adapting LSCPA to Fight or Flight Behavior 65
Summary 67

11. **Building Relationships – Entry, Dialogue and Closure** 69
Entry 71
    Purpose, Process and Payoff (PPP) Statements 71
    Credibility 73
Dialogue 74
    Listening 74
    Exploring 75
    Integrating 76
Closure 78
    Affirming the Agreement 79
    Supporting the Decision 79
    Enhancing the Relationship 80
Building Trust 81
Summary 82

12. **The Social Style Self-Profiler** 84

SECTION 3: SOCIAL STYLES IN DEPTH 88

13. Living and Working with Analyticals 88
Analytical Expectations 89
Entry with Analyticals 93
Dialogue with Analyticals 96
Closure with Analyticals 97
    Affirming 97
    Supporting 98
    Enhancing 99
Adapting Your Style for Analyticals 99
Understanding and Handling Back-Up Behavior
    with Analyticals 103
If You Are an Analytical 104
Summary 105

14. Living and Working with Drivers 107
Driver Expectations 109
Entry with Drivers 112
Dialogue with Drivers 115
Closure with Drivers 115
    Affirming 116
    Supporting 116
    Enhancing 117
Adapting Your Style for Drivers 118
Understanding and Handling Back-Up Behavior
    with Drivers 120
If You Are a Driver 121
Summary 124

15. Living and Working with Amiables 125
Amiable Expectations 128
Entry with Amiables 130
Dialogue with Amiables 131
Closure with Amiables 134
    Affirming 135
    Supporting 135
    Enhancing 136
Adapting Your Style for Amiables 137
Understanding and Handling Back-Up Behavior
    with Amiables 140
If You Are an Amiable 141
Summary 144

16. Living and Working with Expressives 145
Expressive Expectations 146
Entry with Expressives 149

Dialogue with Expressives 150
Closure with Expressives 152
    Affirming 152
    Supporting 153
    Enhancing 154
Adapting Your Style for Expressives 155
Understanding and Handling Back-Up Behavior
    with Expressives 157
If You Are an Expressive 158
Summary 160

SECTION 4: LESSONS FROM SOCIAL STYLES EXPERTS 162

17. Speeding Up the Learning Curve 162
Take It Slowly 163
Don't Jump to Conclusions 164
Stay Away From Stereotypes 165
Be Realistic About the Power of Social Styles 165
Be Aware of Styles Within Styles 166
Accept People's Behavior as a Sign of
    Their Comfort Zones and Nothing More 166
Observe One Dimension of Behavior –
    Assertiveness or Responsiveness – At a Time 167
Observe Verbal and Nonverbal Behaviors –
    and Be Objective 167
Start Assessing Styles Even Before Your First Meeting 168
Use Introductions as Early Indications of Style 169
Focus on Making Only Minor Modifications
    in Your Behavior 170
Live By the Platinum Rule 171
Value Diversity 172
Selling is Easier with Social Styles in Mind 174
Recognize When You Are the One in Back-Up 176
Don't Expect Reciprocity 178
Consistency and Integrity Matter Most 178
Don't Try to Be Someone Else 179

Appendix 180
Resources 183
Contributors 186
Index 188

Foreword

We all know of distinguished doctors whose terrible bedside manners devastate their patients. Or of geniuses in strategic planning who can't inspire anyone to follow their lead. And sadly, we all know partners who give up on love because they can no longer "relate " to one another. What a waste in human potential!

Does this have to be? Daniel Goleman's groundbreaking book *Emotional Intelligence* described this waste, in detail. He argued the cause is a lack of Emotional Intelligence, or EQ – as important as IQ. Only one problem: Daniel didn't tell us *how* to improve our EQ.

Don't despair: *The Social Styles Handbook* has all the how-to answers Daniel left us wondering about, in an easy to understand format. All you have to do is bring your learning attitude.

I believe that weakened or broken relationships are caused by differences in expectations. Think about that for a second now, as it relates to your own relationships at work and at home. In my case, I realized I was so stuck in meeting *my* expectations that I seldom considered the other person's. Ouch! My low EQ kept me from having the strong, productive relationships I wanted.

Then I discovered Social Styles, and I got better. My IQ didn't change, but I upped my EQ. I found more success and fulfillment. You can too.

So learn how to "be" with others by meeting their expectations, making them feel comfortable, and dealing with them on *their* terms. Discover Versatility and the power it brings to your relationships. Learn how to adapt your behavior to the Social Styles of people you want to relate to most.

After you've read and applied *The Social Styles Handbook,* you'll see relationships improve and be more fulfilling, and successes come more easily. If those rewards match *your* expectations, you won't be disappointed. You've already won!

Larry Wilson

Social Style and Versatility

ANALYTICAL
- Focus on facts and logic
- Act when payoff is clear
- Careful not to commit too quickly

DRIVER
- Focus on results
- Take charge
- Make quick decisions
- Like challenges

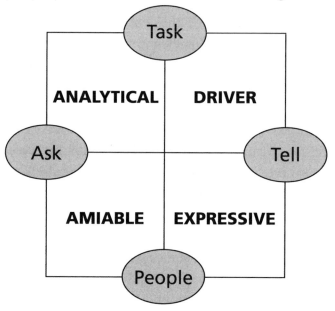

AMIABLE
- Cooperate to gain agreement
- Provide support
- Communicate trust and confidence

EXPRESSIVE
- Create excitement and involvement
- Share ideas, dreams, enthusiasm
- Motivate, inspire, persuade

Research and profiles of more than two million people around the world by Wilson Learning indicate that people fall into one of four Social Styles in terms of their comfort zones of behavior. Roughly 25 percent of the population falls into each group.

THE CASE FOR COMMUNICATION

1 | Introduction

The pure and simple truth is rarely pure and never simple.
OSCAR WILDE

Think about the most important things going on in your life right now. Are you job hunting? Vying for a promotion? In a tough situation with a client, boss or co-worker? Looking to get someone's help, or create a great first impression with someone important? Are you just trying to understand someone who's really different from you? *Wondering why in such everyday situations sometimes you seem to excel, and at other times unravel?*

Think communication. Think relationships.

Strong interpersonal skills won't get you a job for which you have no technical expertise (although we all probably have a story or two to the contrary). You're just as unlikely to get a position for which you are technically qualified, however, if you don't connect on a personal level with a potential new boss. In the big picture of human transaction, people won't buy from you, be influenced by you, or collaborate with you if they aren't comfortable with the way you come across personally and professionally. There are too many choices in the marketplace for most people to be willing to endure excessive tension in professional relationships. Life is too short to spend it working and doing business with people who stress us out.

To get ahead, it helps to get along, and the underpinning of getting along – building strong relationships – is good communication. It's as simple as that. And it's as complicated as that.

Simple? "There is essentially no limit to the number of ideas or propositions that we can convey using sentences," writes Michael Corballis in *American Scientist* magazine. Corballis, a professor of psychology at the University of Auckland in New Zealand, is a noted researcher and author in the area of the origins of language.

Complicated? The remarkable flexibility of human speech, Corballis says, means people can immediately create sentences made up of words perhaps never used in combination before. "Language also allows us to escape from the immediate present and refer to events in other places and at other times," he says. "We can use language to fantasize, to describe events that have never existed and never will."

See where things can start to get thorny?

WORDS AREN'T THE KEY

Further complicating communication, of course, is the research that shows communication – the transfer of information – is based only in small part on the words we use. Albert Mehrabian, professor emeritus at the University of California in Los Angeles and the author of *Silent Messages: Implicit Communication of Emotions and Attitudes*, determined that the effectiveness of communication is based on these three factors:

- 7 percent of the effectiveness of communication is based on the meaning of the words we use.

- 38 percent of the effectiveness is based on the way we say the words we choose.
- 55 percent of the effectiveness is based on nonverbal cues, such as facial expressions.

Although Mehrabian's research was done back in the 1970s, this insight about the disproportional importance of tone of voice and nonverbal signals in communication still surprises many people today. Communication is far trickier than the mere passage of words from one person's lips to another person's ears. Talking is much easier than conveying message and meaning clearly.

Communication is perhaps the most complex thing humans do. It also is arguably the most critical skill for thriving and surviving in just about any situation short of being stranded alone on a desert island. That's why the work of trying to uncover the secrets, mysteries, tips, and tactics of effective communication is an industry unto itself. A search on the Internet for Web sites and resources related to the word "communication" turns up 28 million hits in 0.65 seconds. Refine the search by adding the word "skills" and the number of hits is still 4.3 million. Searches at online booksellers Barnes and Noble and Amazon.com turn up between 35,000 and 62,000 references for books, videos and other learning materials in English.

With all the information about communication that's so readily available, and the prospects that about a million things can go wrong in even the simplest relationships, you may be worrying you'll need your own Ph.D. in psychology to understand what it takes to communicate skillfully. The good news is that *you don't*.

The Social Styles Handbook is based on concepts that are easy to grasp and that reflect the essential wisdom of much of what has been researched and written about improving communication and building successful relationships. No credentials are required for what we have to share with you. All you'll need is a willingness to look at the world a little differently and to adapt your behaviors a bit in the interest of making others more comfortable when you are working on relationships. With practice, what you learn from these pages can make you more effective in just about everything you do that involves others.

SOCIAL STYLES, VERSATILITY AND SUCCESS

Wilson Learning has done nearly 40 years of its own research with more than two million people worldwide in developing and refining our Social Styles tools. We have learned that we can quite accurately group people around the globe into four general Social Styles: Analyticals, Drivers, Expressives and Amiables. We've also learned that simply understanding the implications of these behavior styles is a huge first step in the quest to improve communication and build better relationships. The second step is mastering Versatility, the skill of making slight adjustments in your own behaviors in order to make others more comfortable.

The applications for Social Styles are endless. Look at the list of topics below. Each is a hot-button phrase you'll find in business publications, management books, MBA course catalogs, and, most importantly, on the lists of strategic issues and initiatives in any business operation. Can you find a single topic that isn't greatly influenced by individual skills of communication and relationship building?

- Branding products, services and organizations
- Driving for results and return on investment
- Strategic planning
- Selling in tough times
- Improving quality
- Creating customer loyalty
- Doing more with less
- Creating new markets
- Hiring and retaining great employees
- Leading change
- Creating an environment of innovation

- Working in teams
- Building trust
- Networking for results
- Motivating frontline employees
- Diversifying the work force
- Training the work force
- Leading with integrity
- Driving fear out of the workplace

Wilson Learning research demonstrates that using the Social Styles concepts, tools and techniques can help in all of these big-picture areas, as well as in specialized aspects of professional performance – everything from being a better boss to being a respected and valued team member. The truth is, you could probably easily add to this list almost endlessly.

The science and technology of communication continues to evolve at a staggering pace. The unending parade of new electronic tools – from e-mail to cell phones and Web sites and palm-sized computers – allows us to bombard each other with information from an almost inescapable and growing array of sophisticated methods. Many experts argue, however, that the art of human interaction ultimately plays the most critical role in building solid relationships.

As you work your way through *The Social Styles Handbook*, you will learn about the four Social Styles in detail and begin to understand the foundational implications they have for you and your behavior with others. You will learn your own Social Style and how it influences your success in establishing and maintaining important relationships. You will learn how to "read" other people's styles and adapt your normal behaviors to improve your chances of getting along and performing better. You will gain appreciation for the strengths that each style offers, and benefit from the richness that comes from embracing diversity.

Understanding the case for communication is the beginning. Whether you are a boss wanting to motivate your staff, a salesperson looking to close more deals, or a team member interested in smoothing out how your team works together, the concepts, tools and techniques you will learn in this book can have a profound influence in your life. In the end, you will be better prepared to understand, influence and collaborate with everyone – from co-workers to customers to family and friends. Let's get started.

SUMMARY

- Learning to communicate and build relationships more effectively will influence just about every hot-button aspect of your personal and professional life.
- You don't need a Ph.D. to communicate effectively, just a willingness to look at the world a little differently.
- Only 7 percent of the effectiveness of communication is based on the words we use; everything else is in how we say things.
- The planet divides almost equally into four Social Styles: Analyticals, Drivers, Expressives, and Amiables.
- Versatility is the ability to adapt your behaviors slightly to make others more comfortable.
- Technology provides an extensive array of electronic tools for communicating, but it is the art of human interaction that builds relationships.

2 | Mindset Matters

Convictions are more dangerous enemies of truth than lies.
FRIEDRICH NIETZSCHE

Before we jump into the fascinating subject and applications of Social Styles, we would like you to perform a little exercise. It's a simple physical activity. It will take you less time to complete than it does to read the instructions below. But it will help get you ready for some of the cerebral rearrangements you will make as you learn and use the lessons in *The Social Styles Handbook*.

A WARM-UP EXERCISE
You'll need your hands, so first read these instructions completely, then try it. Then come back, turn the page and continue reading.

The Exercise
1. As illustrated here, fully cross your arms over your chest. You can do this while sitting or standing.
2. One arm will naturally cross over the other. Notice the position of your hands. One is probably on the outside of an arm. Is it your right hand or left? The other hand is probably tucked between your arm and your body. Is it your right hand or your left?

3. Uncross your arms and then cross them again, *but this time, put your other arm on top, with your hands in the opposite positions from when you crossed your arms the first time.* The hand that rested on the outside of your arm the first time should now be tucked between your arm and your chest.

The Point of the Exercise

Did it feel a bit uncomfortable or awkward to cross your arms the second time?

Did you have to stop to think for an instant in order to be sure your hands were in the opposite positions the second time?

If you are like us, and like virtually every person with whom we've ever conducted this exercise, it did take a bit of thinking and readjusting for you to correctly position your hands and arms the second time around. You probably got stuck for a moment.

We've watched many groups of people wrestle with this simple action. Some people quickly cross their arms, then uncross, then pause, physically and mentally… bounce their eyes back and forth from elbow to elbow… partially position one hand… twirl the other over the top… readjust, laugh, pause… and then finish with arms finally locked satisfactorily in place – but sometimes not certain if they have succeeded in switching the overlap as instructed.

Here is why we asked you to do this exercise. We all have ways of saying and doing things that are most comfortable and natural. We cross our arms dozens of times a day without ever thinking about how to do it, and most people do it similarly every time. The same is true about how we communicate. At times, using Social Styles will cause you similar confusion and discomfort. Using Social Styles also may sometimes require the same kind of awkward, stop-for-a-moment-and-think assessment of a situation in order for you to put all the right pieces in the right places. It requires conscious effort, at least at first. Practice will make things feel more natural, however.

People who naturally come on strong with a firm handshake, commanding voice and direct eye contact when meeting someone new tend to use the same grip and greeting with everyone. It's habit. It's easiest. As you will see as you progress through *The Social Styles Handbook*, however, research shows that the communication style with which you are most comfortable will be a mismatch with the majority of people you meet. What's comfortable for you will not be comfortable for them. And that hinders communication and relationships.

ESSENTIAL MINDSETS

You'll need to adopt a few critically important mindsets as you work through this book.

Mindset #1: Look for the signals and respond correctly

Once you make yourself aware of the different behaviors associated with the four Social Styles, you will find that with three out of four people, you will have to do things that might not seem easy or natural in order to communicate effectively. When you begin to understand and read others' Social Styles clues and cues, you'll pick up messages about how to behave. Be ready for them, and know that with a little practice, you will get better at handling them.

Mindset #2: Be prepared to act in ways that don't feel comfortable

This mindset builds on the first one: Once you are aware that differences in Social Styles can create problems in communicating and building relationships, it's essential to realize you have the choice of whether to use that knowledge wisely.

It's important to recognize when someone else's communication style doesn't match yours, but pointing a finger at the source of conflict doesn't make that conflict go away.

Imagine yourself belted into the seat of a commercial airliner, stuck on a hot runway as the result of an air traffic delay. In the seat next to you is a man in a business suit, who, as the minutes pass, becomes increasingly agitated, angry, and unhappy about the wait. Finally, he reaches the point where he can't contain his displeasure. Tevilla Riddell, a consultant in the Wilson Learning Extended Enterprise, has been in this exact position.

"Here was a guy, in all his expressiveness, loudly letting everyone around him know how unhappy he was. He was creating a huge drama out of the situation. Without knowing what I know about Social Styles," Tevilla says, "my first reaction might have been to think, 'What a jerk!'

"Knowing Social Styles, I understood that I just had to be patient with this man. He was upset and his outspoken behavior was his way of dealing with it. In a situation like this, it was my choice how I reacted to him. I could be patient, or I could go with the first instinctive – and negative – reaction many of us might have with someone like this. I'm certain there would have only been more conflict if I hadn't adapted by understanding his style-driven response to the tension.

"I laugh to myself sometimes when I overhear people getting upset in restaurants, on airplanes, and in other public situations; it just makes me want to tell the whole world about Social Styles. . . to show people that there are other ways to communicate in tough situations."

Seeing the difference in Social Styles isn't enough for you to improve your communication and build more successful relationships, however. In fact, when some people first learn about Social Styles, they become overly fascinated with being able to figure out other people's styles, and they forget the true value of that understanding. When there are differences between people, someone has to make a change to accommodate those differences or else communication will suffer. Social Styles provides the wherewithal for you to take the lead on the never-ending challenge of accomodating differences.

Mindset #3: You can't change your own style, but you can adapt your behavior

Using Social Styles does not require you change who you are, what you believe, or how you feel about important issues, nor does it suggest you should be manipulative, deceitful, or dishonest in any way. In fact, extensive research shows that it is extremely difficult and highly unlikely for most of us to change our Social Styles, and attempts to be untrue to ourselves or to deceive others about who we most often prove to be counterproductive in building relationships.

James Miller, a software development manager for Qwest, a major phone service provider based in Denver, Colorado in the US, puts it simply and clearly. He says his many years of using Social Styles have shown that "Social Styles is not a trick or a gimmick."

Indeed, it's critical to approach Social Styles with a genuine interest and concern for the people with whom you communicate. To do otherwise is to run the risk of damaging your credibility and undermining trust, both of which are essential to successful relationships.

French playwright and novelist Jean Giraudoux once said, "The secret of success is sincerity. Once you can fake that you've got it made." Again, we all probably know a few people who miss the irony in a statement like this and go through life trying to "fake it."

Applying the techniques of Social Styles requires sincerity – genuine sincerity, not faked. Using Social Styles requires learning and using new behavior. It does *not* require a major personal overhaul.

Mindset #4: Diversity is enriching, but requires understanding

The world's economic and geographic boundaries are becoming increasingly porous. There's little doubt that, as a result of this change, all the important things going on in your life are bringing you into contact with a much more diverse set of personal and professional contacts. As you will quickly see, your ability to communicate more effectively and to build better relationships in all situations will improve dramatically as you learn to make the slight-but-crucial Social Style adjustments in your behaviors in order to make other people more comfortable.

SUMMARY

As you head into the next chapters explaining Social Styles in detail, you may have to let go of a few convictions, habits, and things you've always done in order to become better at communicating and building relationships. Your mindset matters:

- Be ready for the awkward moments when it will make you a bit uncomfortable to interact in response to different Social Styles. Just like crossing your arms unnaturally, it may take a little thought to get it right.
- Identifying Social Styles differences in others is not enough; you've got to adapt your behavior in response to what you observe.
- One secret of Social Styles success is sincerity. You can modify your behaviors in response to behavior differences without compromising or changing who you are.
- When you fully understand the four Social Styles, you gain appreciation for the unique ways in which people behave and can make the most of this diversity.

DIMENSIONS
OF SOCIAL STYLES

---

3 | A New View of Behavior

Common sense is the collection of prejudices acquired by age eighteen.

ALBERT EINSTEIN

Sherry Schoolcraft has facilitated Social Styles learning events as a member of the Wilson Learning Extended Enterprise since the 1980s. Her immediate reaction when she was first exposed to the concepts was, "Wow. This makes so many of my life experiences make perfect sense."

The concepts "addressed things that I understood intuitively to some extent," she says, "but they gave me terminology and skills I didn't have. I saw immediately this was something that was going to help me deal more successfully with relationships in all parts of my life – personal and professional."

As Sherry and most of the 2 million other people around the world who have learned the Social Styles tools could quickly see, Social Styles provides a new way to look at the world. There is a language that goes along with Social Styles that will require you to learn some new terms – or at least to consider new meanings for terms with which you may already be familiar. There is much to learn in the details. In the end, however, Social Styles comes down to helping you answer three essential questions:

1. What is my Social Style?
2. What are the Social Styles of the important people in my life?
3. What adjustments do I have to make in my behavior to make things go better with these people?

TWO CRITICAL ASSUMPTIONS

We make two critical assumptions that you need to have clearly in mind as you begin to explore with us the details and these essential questions underlying Social Styles, dealing with behavior and reality.

Social Style focuses only on observable behavior

Social Style does not assess intelligence or aptitude, nor does it interpret personality or character. It does not evaluate performance or correctness. Social Style doesn't help you delve into people's heads or hearts. You can never know for sure what a customer, a boss, a co-worker, or even a dear friend is thinking or feeling. But watch and listen closely; you *can* see and hear what they're doing and saying. Those actions tell and show you what it will take to earn their trust, confidence, and willingness to build a relationship with you.

Perception is reality

What we see is what we believe. Unfortunately what we infer from what we see isn't always true. It will take practice using Social Styles for you to increase your awareness, improve your powers of observation, and sharpen your ability to draw accurate conclusions about the significance of other people's behaviors.

Perhaps more important, your perceptions of yourself and your own Social Style may not match what others see. Although the key people in your life may not know Social Styles, they nonetheless are making judgments about, and reacting to, your behaviors with them. Ultimately, your Social Style is how others see you, not how you see yourself.

In fact, often the way we see ourselves differs from how others see us. But the majority of participants in Social Styles programs come to agree on the profile given by people they interact with who are asked to describe them. James Miller learned this lesson early on in his first experience with Social Styles over 10 years ago. He has carried the learning with him into his manager of software development position at Qwest, a major phone service provider based in Denver, Colorado in the US. He didn't completely agree initially with his co-workers' perception of his Social Style when they did group assessments of each other, but he has figured out that he "can live with that," and has adapted his behavior accordingly.

Learning and using the Social Style matrix can open your eyes to new ways of seeing things, help reduce the tension that can threaten relationships, and make you more successful at just about anything you do that involves communication – which is a lot. Mastery will take patience, practice persistence, and solid comprehension of the terms and models that come next.

SUMMARY
Social Styles concepts help you identify the ways people perceive your natural style of communication and the natural styles of other people.

* Learning and using Social Style comes down to answering three questions: What style am I? What are the styles of the important people in my life? How can I behave to make things go better with these people?
* You can use your knowledge of Social Styles to modify your behavior and enhance the ways you communicate with others.
* Social Styles deals with observable behavior, not feelings, thoughts or intuition.
* Perception is reality. Your Social Style is how others see you, not how you see yourself.

4 | Assertiveness and Responsiveness – The Measures of Behavior

While it is the camel at the front of the caravan that holds everything up,
it is the ones at the back that get the beating.
ETHIOPIAN PROVERB

Social scientists of every ilk – from sociologists to psychologists – have conducted extensive research on human behavior for decades. They have come up with a wide array of terms and methodologies to define, classify, measure, describe, and categorize what they have learned about the various ways people interact.

ASSERTIVENESS AND RESPONSIVENESS

At Wilson Learning, we've conducted nearly 40 years of study on Social Styles. In our work, we have identified two dimensions of interpersonal actions that cut across much of the research done worldwide, and that encompass all the major behavioral tendencies we see in each other: *assertiveness and responsiveness.*

It is very important to understand these two terms because they form the foundation of the Social Style matrix. We will take each one up in turn.

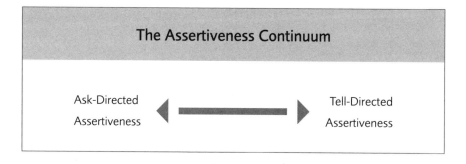

The Assertiveness Continuum

Ask-Directed
Assertiveness

Tell-Directed
Assertiveness

Assertiveness – the measure of influencing

Assertiveness refers to the way in which we are perceived as trying to influence the thoughts and actions of others.

Everybody is assertive. We all spend a lot of time and energy trying to get what we want, but we do it differently. If you view assertiveness as being measured on a left-to-right continuum, the left end of the scale *is ask-directed* and the right end is *tell-directed.*

People on the ask-directed end of the scale tend to be more subtle and indirect in the way they try to influence others. They ask more questions and tend to suggest or offer ideas rather than make strong declarative statements or present conclusions. The nonverbal cues you get from ask-directed people are also subtler. They lean back in their chairs when they speak. They tend to talk more slowly, allow pauses, and most often appear calm and composed.

People on the tell-directed end of the scale tend to be more up front and demonstrative in their statements and body language. They typically speak at a faster pace and often take quick initiative to keep conversations and plans moving. The nonverbal cues from the tell-directed people also are usually more direct. You'll see them leaning forward during your conversations, and everything will sound a bit louder and faster.

Research clearly shows there is no "best place" on this continuum of assertiveness. Although we've only just begun to scratch the surface in explaining Social Styles, you may already be thinking about where you and others fall on this scale. Great. But don't worry about being

Assertiveness Behaviors	
Ask-Directed	**Tell-Directed**
Speaks deliberately, often pausing	Speaks quickly and often firmly
Seldom interrupts others	Often interrupts others
Seldom uses voice for emphasis	Often uses voice for emphasis
Makes many conditional statements	Makes many declarative statements
Tends to lean back	Tends to lean forward

"right or wrong" or "better or worse." There's no research that demonstrates those who ask more or tell more have a distinctive advantage in influencing others.

The research does show, however, that depending on the situation, some assertiveness behaviors will be more effective than others when it comes to building productive relationships. Learning Social Styles will help you identify the opportunities to modify your own behavior along the assertiveness continuum so that you influence others in the way that is most comfortable and acceptable to them. Naturally, this should increase your ability to influence them.

As you begin to use Social Styles to understand others and modify your behavior to improve communication, one of the first things you'll do is observe whether others are more or less tell-directed or ask-directed than yourself.

Responsiveness – the measure of expressing

Responsiveness refers to the way in which we are perceived when expressing our feelings when relating to others.

There are also two ends to the continuum on responsiveness. Because this characteristic is independent of assertiveness, we think of this measurement scale as flowing top to bottom. People whose Social Style is in the upper part of the continuum are *task-directed*. Those whose Social Style is *people-directed* are at the lower part. In general, people-directed types find it more important to be able to express their feelings in their interactions than those who are task-directed.

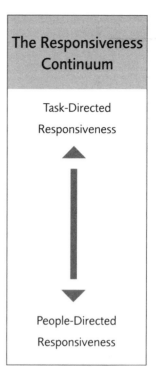

The Responsiveness Continuum

Task-Directed
Responsiveness

People-Directed
Responsiveness

Contrary to what some people instinctively infer or assume from this scale, people who are task-directed and people who are people-directed all experience the full range of human feelings; they just express themselves differently in relation to tasks and the people.

People who are *task-directed* are usually more reserved in expressing their emotions. Their preference in most situations is to focus first on the task at hand rather than sharing their personal feelings or talking about their personal issues. Only after work issues have been dealt with will they take up interpersonal topics. They will tend to talk more about the facts of a project than about the people involved with it. And their nonverbal clues tend toward a composed posture, level tone of voice, contained gestures, and limited facial expressions.

Those individuals on the other end of this continuum – the *people-directed* side – generally express their emotions quite openly and freely. They are often inclined to focus on the feelings and relationship issues that are tied into a task at hand, often believing that task issues are easier to deal with after they have established personal relationships. They talk frequently about the people on their project teams, their working relationships, and building cooperation. When communicating nonverbally, those who are people-directed use broad and varied gestures, a variable tone of voice, and more facial expressions.

Responsiveness Behaviors	
Task-Directed	**People-Directed**
Talks more about tasks and facts	Talks more about people and relationships
Uses minimal body gestures	Uses broad, expansive body gestures
Shows a narrow range of personal feelings to others	Shows a broad range of personal feelings to others
Uses limited facial expressions	Uses varied and open facial expressions

Again, it's critically important not to attach any judgment of character or effectiveness to these behavioral descriptors. There is no right or wrong responsiveness type, no right or wrong assertiveness type. There is no better or worse, just different. We all know people on all ends of the continua who are effective and successful in their work.

Assertiveness and Responsiveness – the basis for the Social Style matrix

To create the four-block grid we call the Social Style matrix, we combine the assertiveness and responsiveness continua so they cross at a midpoint. You will find much more detail on the matrix as you read the upcoming chapters, but here are the basics:

Right or Left – People who are more tell-directed land to the right of the midpoint on the matrix; those who are ask-directed land to the left.

Above or Below – People who are task-directed land above the midpoint, while those who are people-directed land below the midpoint.

The crossed lines of the two continua create the four quadrants of Social Styles. In the Social Style matrix:

- People who fall in the upper-left quadrant (ask-directed, task-directed) are identified as *Analyticals*.
- People in the upper-right quadrant (tell-directed, task-directed) are identified as *Drivers*.

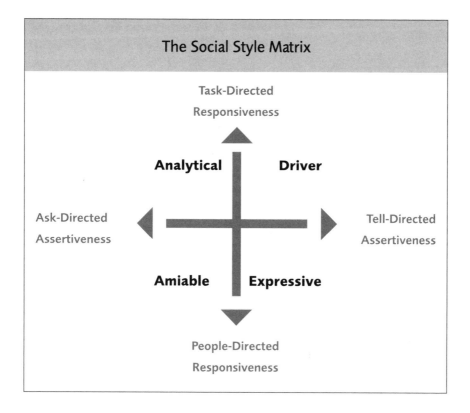

- People in the lower-left quadrant (ask-directed, people-directed) are *Amiables*.
- People in the lower-right quadrant (tell-directed, people-directed) are *Expressives*.

No two people – even those who share the same Social Style – behave the same way in all situations. A fundamental truth about Social Styles, however, is that you are far more likely to connect quickly and most easily with other people whose behavior falls in the same quadrant as yours.

The population actually divides roughly into equal numbers of Analyticals, Drivers, Amiables and Expressives. You'll learn more about determining your own behavior style in Chapter 12, where you'll use the Social Style Profiler, and in Section 3, Social Styles In Depth. But

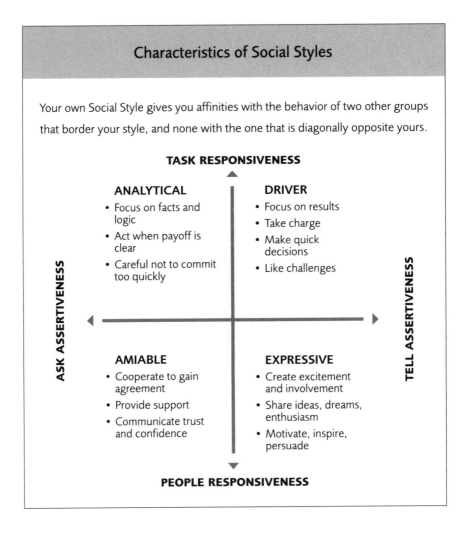

Characteristics of Social Styles

Your own Social Style gives you affinities with the behavior of two other groups that border your style, and none with the one that is diagonally opposite yours.

TASK RESPONSIVENESS

ANALYTICAL
- Focus on facts and logic
- Act when payoff is clear
- Careful not to commit too quickly

DRIVER
- Focus on results
- Take charge
- Make quick decisions
- Like challenges

ASK ASSERTIVENESS

TELL ASSERTIVENESS

AMIABLE
- Cooperate to gain agreement
- Provide support
- Communicate trust and confidence

EXPRESSIVE
- Create excitement and involvement
- Share ideas, dreams, enthusiasm
- Motivate, inspire, persuade

PEOPLE RESPONSIVENESS

whatever your style, this demographic breakdown means you've got a great deal in common with about 25 percent of the people you meet. You are similar to them on both dimensions of behavior – assertiveness and responsiveness.

This breakdown also means you've got at least something in common with 50 percent of the remaining population; your quadrant in the matrix shares sides with two other styles. You are similar in either your assertiveness or your responsiveness to people whose behavior falls in those adjacent quadrants.

Shared Behavior Among Social Style Groups

Social Style	Share Assertiveness (Ask vs. Tell) Behavior with:	Share Responsiveness (Task vs. People) Behavior with:	Share No Behavior with:
Analyticals	Amiables	Drivers	Expressives
Drivers	Expressives	Analyticals	Amiables
Amiables	Analyticals	Expressives	Drivers
Expressives	Drivers	Amiables	Analytical s

For your particular Social Style, two other style groups have similarities and one does not. For example, if you are an Expressive, you are tell-directed on the assertiveness dimension and people-directed on the responsiveness dimension. That means you share assertive behavior styles with Drivers because you both are tell-directed. You share responsive behavior styles with Amiables because you are both people-directed. You don't share any styles of behavior with Analyticals – speaking here in terms of your respective natural comfort zones, not your ability to adapt and move towards theirs.

That leaves 25 percent of the population, of course, with whom you share no similarities in assertive or responsive behaviors. Wherever you land on the matrix, these are the people in the quadrant that is diagonally across from yours. No sides of your quadrant touch the sides of this group's quadrant. Your assertive and responsive behaviors are actually diametrically opposed. Not surprisingly, this is the group with whom you may have the greatest difficulty communicating comfortably.

SUMMARY

- The two most-telling measures of interpersonal behavior are assertiveness (how we influence) and responsiveness (how we express feelings related to tasks and people).

- The assertiveness continuum is represented by a horizontal line with ask-assertiveness on the left and tell-assertiveness on the right.
- The responsiveness continuum is represented by a vertical line with task-responsiveness at the top and people-responsiveness at the bottom.
- When superimposed, the two continua form the Social Styles Matrix. The resulting quadrants are labeled Analytical (ask-task driven styles), Driver (task-tell driven styles), Amiable (ask-people driven styles) and Expressive (tell-people driven styles).
- There is a sort of natural comfort for people dealing with others who share the same Social Style. People feel somewhat less comfortable with others whose Social Styles place them in the two quadrants that share only one side with someone else's. People feel least comfortable and natural with others whose Social Style quadrant is diagonally across from their own, because they share no similarities in style.
- The population divides almost equally among the four quadrants, meaning you have only one chance in four, statistically, of sharing styles with another person.
- People often think they come across differently from the way others perceive them.

5 | Versatility – Adapting Your Style

I don't have an attitude problem.
You have a perception problem.
DILBERT, A COMIC STRIP CHARACTER CREATED BY SCOTT ADAMS

Perception problems underlie much of what goes wrong in communication, and therefore in relationships.

The trouble happens on two levels:

First, what we see is what we believe, but what we say to ourselves about what we see isn't always true.

Second, as we said earlier, the way we see ourselves isn't always the way others see us; often what we think we are projecting is different from the way we come across in relationships.

As you begin to understand where others land on the assertiveness and responsiveness scales and in the four quadrants of the Social Style matrix, you'll become increasingly aware that the problem when communication fails is not that others are trying to mislead us, or that we are trying to fool others. In fact, everything we do and say provides honest clues about who we are and what makes us most comfortable in relationships. Things break down most often when those signs are misread, or not read at all. Social Style tools help you interpret those clues and gain insights into other people's preferences about how they want to interact. With them, you can learn to be Versatile and see dramatic improvements in your relationships.

VERSATILITY IN ACTION

Versatility is the skill of using those insights. It comes into play when you:

- Recognize that the differences between your and other people's Social Styles are causing problems in your communication and relationships.
- Decide you want to behave differently to make your communication and relationships better.

Versatility is your willingness and ability to make temporary adjustments in your assertiveness and responsiveness styles. The extent to which you are versatile is a critical factor in your ability to begin, build and sustain relationships.

COMFORT ZONES – YOURS AND THEIRS

Joyce Jappelle, a facilitator and consultant in the Wilson Learning Extended Enterprise, says, "When I am conscious of Social Styles and my own Versatility in professional and personal situations, I am quite effective. That's when things go really well.

"When I'm not conscious of being versatile it's easy to slip back into a comfort zone that feels good to me but that doesn't always work for other people. It's those times, when I end a phone call or a meeting, for example, feeling as if I missed a real opportunity.

"When I'm not being versatile, my clients may not literally see me rolling my eyes skeptically in response to something they say, but in my mind I am rolling them. I'm saying to myself, 'Why are they saying that? What are they thinking?'

"If I'm being versatile, and conscious of what I'm doing, I can get beyond that reaction and adjust my behavior so the client feels comfortable."

At times when the economy was booming and business was plentiful, Joyce says, it might not have been so critical to be vigilant about

Versatility. "In the mid-1990s I could have accepted projects that would have me working 24 hours a day. In those days, if I didn't think I could connect with a client or if I thought it might be too difficult to make a relationship work, I would turn down business. In today's economy it's rare to be able to afford to do that. I depend on Versatility to understand and improve relationships."

As we have pointed out before, Versatility pays off in every imaginable type of relationship, from doctor to patient, boss to staffer, consultant to client, mother to daughter, and everything in between.

SUMMARY

- The Social Styles tool provides insights into human behaviors, and Versatility is the skill used to adjust your own behavior in response to others' needs.
- Using Versatility requires that you *recognize* which Social Style differences are operating in your relationships and *decide* to behave differently to make your relationships better.
- Versatility has implications for every imaginable type of relationship. Diligence is required to make this skill pay off.

6 | Task and Relationship Tension – Productive or Unproductive?

"I highly recommend worrying. It's much more effective than dieting."
WILLIAM POWELL

One of the key objectives of using Versatility is to manage tension in a relationship.

Although we tend to think of all tension as a source of negative stress, that's not really the case. It's more helpful to think of tension as being productive or unproductive.

There are two kinds of tension in every relationship – task tension and relationship tension. It's perhaps easiest to envision these two tension factors by thinking about a particular type of relationship.

TASK TENSION

Imagine you are a project manager responsible for the delivery, installation and servicing of new office equipment purchased from your company by a multinational organization opening a new location in Warsaw. There are deadlines to meet. There are financial implications to take into account. There are last-minute order changes to handle, as well as onsite crises related to people unhappy with their new accommodations. There are reputations, personal pride, guarantees, and plenty of money at stake. People are counting on your client to make good decisions. All of these factors create a sense of urgency for your client to be smart, thrifty, thorough, and to hold you accountable for getting the new space operational as quickly and efficiently as possible.

That's task tension.

Although it may not be quite as easy to pinpoint task tension in some situations, it exists in virtually every relationship. If you are part of a work team assigned to a special project, the same kinds of goal and deadline pressures exist. If you are interviewing for a promotion or a new job, you and the person doing the interview both want to get through the process as effectively as possible – the interviewer needs help and you want a new career opportunity. Or, if you're trying to get your family focused on cleaning up the house before company arrives for a holiday celebration, there are things to be done by a deadline. A similar sort of tension drives you and others to get all these different sorts of tasks done.

RELATIONSHIP TENSION

Relationship tension is just as natural a part of any communication process as task tension, but it results much more from the personal connection – or lack of it – between you and others.

In the project management situation described above, for example, the client who bought the furniture for that new corporate headquarters may not feel a high level of trust with you in the initial stages of the delivery and installation. That lack of trust doesn't mean the client has a low opinion of you; more likely it's just a matter of that person not knowing enough about you and how you will handle this project. That uncertainty about who you are and how you operate creates relationship tension.

Relationship tension is not only present at the beginning of a relationship, however. In a sales situation, it can resurface at any point if you are not aware of the dynamics of the interaction. As you begin to uncover customers' needs, they might feel an increase in relationship tension if it's not perfectly clear you fully understand the problems and expectations unique to their situations. Relationship tension also can increase when you reach the point of influencing a final buying decision, and again after the buying decision is made. Those are the moments when customers' concerns often mount about implementation and resolution of the problems the purchase is targeted to solve.

Again, the same is true in every kind of relationship. If you look, you will find evidence of tension in virtually all your connections with friends, co-workers, customers, strangers on the street, clerks behind counters, or family members. Relationship tension doesn't serve much positive purpose. Task tension, on the other hand, can be productive in relationships because it can help keep the participants motivated about doing what needs to be done together.

RISING AND FALLING TENSION

As you work with Social Styles, you will also notice that tension levels vary at different stages in any given relationship. An important aspect of Versatility is recognizing, or even orchestrating, these shifts, and then adjusting your behavior to make the tension work for you, not against you.

Early in a group project, for example, task tension may be relatively low if your team's deadlines are quite far off. The details of what must be accomplished may be just beginning to become clear. Other people who may have future significant roles to play related to the project may not yet be fully engaged. Likewise, the first time you meet with a new boss to discuss job responsibilities, the sense of urgency about the new role you will be playing may also be relatively low.

To make task tension work to the advantage of a relationship, sometimes it may need to be heightened. A little extra productive stress can contribute a lot of extra energy for keeping yourself and others focused, attentive, and moving toward your goals. Most likely, accomplishing your goals in a relationship will also require that you periodically turn down or turn off relationship tension.

Put simply, relationship tension is unproductive because it suppresses task tension. Task tension can be extremely beneficial if it is a healthy expression of the urgency and willingness to get down to the task at hand, but stress on the interpersonal level tends to get in the way of being able to collaborate on tasks.

As you learn about each Social Style in detail, you'll discover that people in some quadrants of the Social Style matrix make decisions more slowly than others. Drivers generally make decisions quickly and independently, for example, while Analyticals usually require extra time, extensive facts, figures and details before reaching conclusions. If you are in a relationship with one Driver and one Analytical and one of your goals is to agree on a timely decision, you may have to find ways to increase task tension for the Analytical to conclude the research stage and come to resolution. You might also have to decrease task tension a bit for the Driver in order to provide at least some of the additional time needed by the Analytical. And in both cases, you will have to be mindful of not increasing relationship tension for either of these people in the process.

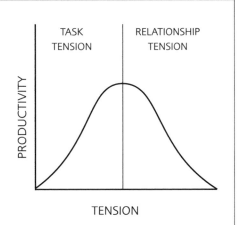

Task and Relationship Tension and Productivity

A certain amount of task tension is good. It increases productivity directed toward the goal you are accomplishing together with others in a relationship. Relationship tension prevents people from focusing on task tension. When relationship tension is high, people become uncomfortable and task-directed productivity drops

MOVING FROM RELATIONSHIP TO TASK TENSION

A challenge in building productive relationships is to move away from relationship tension as fast as possible so you can focus together on managing the task tension productively. There are a lot of things to get done in any relationship. You don't want interpersonal stress to detract from those tasks.

Earlier we said relationship tension often can be highest at the beginning of a relationship. It can be beneficial to recognize and address this situation immediately. But even after initial relationship tension is lessened, you must constantly watch out for an increase or recurrence. It's not unusual for people to have moments when they feel angry or

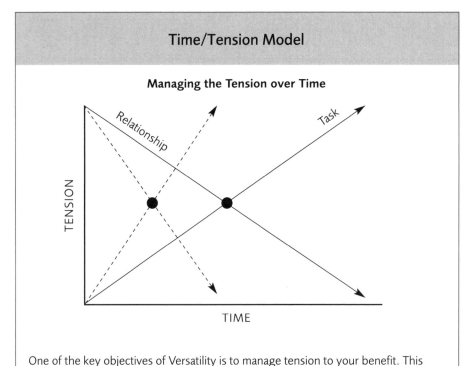

Time/Tension Model

Managing the Tension over Time

Relationship

Task

TENSION

TIME

One of the key objectives of Versatility is to manage tension to your benefit. This means reducing or eliminating relationship tension as quickly as you can, because it suppresses task tension and inhibits collaboration. When relationship tension drops, task tension rises and encourages productivity.

frustrated, or suddenly go quiet. Even in close personal or professional relationships, tension levels can become intense unexpectedly and result in shouting matches or extended bouts of silence. If you have teenage children (or remember what it was like to be a teenager) you know exactly what we mean.

These responses to uncomfortably high tension are part of human interaction, and they are important indicators about tension levels and relationship status. They offer unique insights and require special handling, both of which you'll learn more about in upcoming chapters.

SUMMARY

- Tension can be productive or unproductive in any relationship.
- Task tension is productive because it moves people along in accomplishing goals.
- Relationship tension is unproductive because it suppresses your ability to focus on the task.
- You can use Social Styles techniques to reduce initial relationship tension quickly so task tension can rise.
- Due to any number of factors, relationship tension may rise again in the course of a project or relationship. Again, Social Styles techniques can help address and reduce it and return people to making progress on their tasks or goals.

7 | Comfort – The Key to Trust and Confidence

We all have comfort zones several sizes too small.

UNKNOWN

The ability to make others feel comfortable is the essence of Versatility.

The great communicators in the world, the people you know and admire for their aptitude at nurturing strong relationships, all have a knack for putting people at ease.

COMFORT OPENS THE WAY TO TRUST

With comfort comes trust and confidence, which are prerequisites for being able to move any relationship beyond the superficial and get things done with others.

Without trust, your colleagues or customers won't disclose the information you need to work with them. They won't be receptive to your suggestions. And they simply won't do what you request. That's true whether your customer is a client purchasing legal services from you or a colleague from your company's marketing team to whom you must sell your ideas for a new product introduction.

Without trust, co-workers or people you supervise will be leery of hidden meanings in what you say. You've seen it many times – there will be more energy spent on debating the politics and intentions of various players than on the work at hand. These days, nobody has time for that.

THE EFFECTS OF DISCOMFORT

As you learned in reading about task and relationship tension, when others experience excessive stress in their relationships with you, the energy needed to get things done is dissipated by their personal discomfort. Without comfort, your relationships are likely to falter and your performance in anything you do involving other people will fall short of everybody's expectations.

Tevilla Riddell remembers immediately thinking about uncomfortable relationships with co-workers when she first learned about Social Styles. "I was looking for immediate applications for what I was learning and I remember saying, 'Now I understand the misconnections.' I realized the issue wasn't about people liking or disliking me; it was a matter of them having different needs in terms of communication."

"I found that application right away," Tevilla says, "and now I use it all the time, whether it's with clients on a sales call or dropping off my laundry at the dry cleaner's. This awareness about people feeling discomfort gives me an effective strategy for looking at how I approach relationships. It makes me stop and ask myself, 'What can I do to improve communication?'"

The key phrase, of course, is, "What can I do to improve communication?"

In other words, what can you do to make other people feel more comfortable, even if it means making yourself somewhat uncomfortable in the process?

It is critical to understand that Versatility doesn't mean adjusting your behaviors to make yourself comfortable in every communication situation. On the contrary, being versatile and successful in building productive relationships means, at times, you purposefully take on a degree of discomfort for yourself. And this is a reality that may never change. No matter how well you master Social Styles, there will probably always be situations that challenge you to adjust your own comfort zone in the interest of accommodating the communication needs of others.

THE PAYOFFS FOR MAKING OTHERS COMFORTABLE

The implications for the benefits of focusing on the comfort of others in your relationships are apparent in countless daily situations.

In a coaching or managing situation, if you don't happen to share the other person's Social Style, your most carefully constructed positive criticism and guidance may not hit the mark, if the other person feels too much discomfort. Trust will be lower and a degree of defensiveness may even develop.

If you work on a team of people who all happen to share a given Social Style, it's easy to forget that when you make a presentation to an outside group that the members of that group may be from different styles, or even from various different styles. Making a conscious effort to pitch your communication with the audience's styles in mind can really produce good results here.

In any customer situation, assuring your customer's comfort will pay off in many ways. Among other things, it will help you get a better sense of what it will take to develop a long-term relationship that can translate into repeat business.

Ann Horner, a main board director at Bourne Leisure Limited in the UK, makes extensive use of Social Styles in this regard. Bourne Leisure sells caravans (trailer homes) and holiday stays at a range of holiday resort locations across the UK and Europe. One of the numerous applications and benefits of Social Styles, for Ann, is to make others comfortable. This ranges from very personal and practical to organizational and strategic levels.

It's not her tendency to write down many of the ideas and plans she discusses with colleagues, Ann says. "I often also go with my gut feeling on things, but I have some colleagues who are more comfortable when we do more analysis. Because I value the differences in our styles, I've learned to put more things on paper and to not rush those colleagues' decisions, which leaves them time to come up with options I might not have thought of. It has been good for me to create this kind of self-discipline."

As a company, Ann says, Bourne Leisure uses Social Styles and an overriding concern about the comfort of others in hiring practices and in making other strategic personnel decisions.

"Bourne Leisure is the epitome of a versatile company," she says. "We have incredible diversity, starting with the founding partners," who deliberately cultivate and regularly exploit the differences in their own styles. "We have strong role models for hiring people to support our weaknesses and take advantage of differences. As an organization, we are quick to identify the skills people need to deal with the problems they will face in certain positions.

"Relationships are critical in any business, but we have 40 resorts with a variety of facilities, and we operate with remote staff that might be 10 hours' travel time away from us. Relationships are really important for us. When we decide who will run a particular park, we think about who has the style best suited for that location, and we think about the preferences our people have for what they want to do and how they want to do it."

The practice of focusing on the other person's comfort might seem excessive or operationally risky to some businesspeople. However, just as focusing on another person's comfort in a one-to-one relationship can create trust, confidence, collaboration and results, so can a management team's willingness to be a bit uncomfortable in its leadership practices.

"If you focus on the outcomes you're after," Ann says, "you see there is a much bigger potential payoff if you're willing to work on your own Versatility. It is just so helpful to look at things from your customer's perspective . . . and to understand that *everyone* you work with is a customer.

"We know we can't just tell people in our organization what to do. If you accept that, you realize you have to put yourself in their shoes and to think about what's in it for them to do what you need done, and to think about what will be the most comfortable and effective ways for them to deal with those issues."

THE REQUIREMENTS FOR COMFORT

Creating comfort for others will require different things from you in different situations.

As you have already discovered, there are four main Social Styles that you will learn about in detail in the upcoming chapters – Analytical, Expressive, Amiable and Driver. You will find that you fit best in one of those four styles of communication.

As you have also learned, statistically speaking, one out of every four of people you meet will be the same Social Style as you. In those cases the same behaviors might make you both comfortable. In three out of four cases, however, the things that might help you feel comfortable are not likely to have the same effect for the other person in a relationship.

For some people, you will have to adjust your assertiveness to make them more comfortable, and for others, you will have to modify your responsiveness. For those in the Social Styles quadrant diagonally across from yours, you will need to adjust on both dimensions. Not surprisingly, this is the group with whom you may have the greatest difficulty communicating comfortably. All of this means, of course, you may have to stretch your own comfort zone to make the majority of your relationships more successful. You can hope for reciprocity; the best possible scenario for building great relationships is when all parties are willing to make adjustments to help others feel comfortable. The reality, however, is that you may be operating on your own most of the time, and it's up to you to recognize that your success with using Social Styles depends on your willingness to focus on making others comfortable without worrying about your own comfort levels.

You can have a huge influence on the relationships in your life, even when you are interacting with people who seem to have little or no intuitive awareness of the Social Style concepts. The detailed look at the characteristics and behaviors of the four Social Styles you will learn in Section 3 will build on this fundamental concept that good relationships begin with comfort.

SUMMARY

- Making others – not yourself – feel comfortable is the essence of Versatility.
- Comfort inspires trust and confidence, without which there is not much chance of creating and maintaining a successful relationship.
- The payoffs for making others comfortable range from earning repeat business from customers to building an organizational culture that empowers and enables people to perform at the highest possible levels.
- Making others comfortable will require you to stretch your own comfort zone in three out of four relationships. Sometimes you will need to adjust your assertiveness, at other times your responsiveness, and with people in the Social Style quadrant diagonally opposite yours, both.

8 | Habit – Getting Beyond Comfort and Custom in Communication

If you find yourself in a hole,
the first thing is to stop diggin'.
WILL ROGERS

We are all creatures of habit.

Dee Hock, the founder of credit card giant VISA, once said, "The problem is never how to get new, innovative thoughts into your mind, but how to get old ones out."

This insight is significant to Social Styles for a number of reasons. First, of course, we are asking you to consider communicating differently. Whether you are 20 or 64, you have been managing your relationships in your own way for all those years. And you have no doubt been quite successful at it.

Our promise is that you can be even more successful. But to do so you must make room in your thinking for some new ideas related to Social Styles, in part at least, by giving up of some of your old ideas and behaviors. That is often not easy to do.

COMFORT ZONES AND HABITS

One reason that it is hard to give them up is comfort, as discussed in Chapter 7. But you are also influenced by habit.

We all have our comfort zones that define the patterns we follow and the boundaries we impose in doing the routine things in our lives. We know people who automatically put on the same shoe first every time they dress, and almost feel compelled to start over if they inadvertently mix up the order. It's a little thing. It's comfortable that way. It's easy. It's something done with little or no thought. It's a habit.

Putting on the same shoe first every day is not a behavior that will influence anything of much importance in your life. Most of us, though, also have comfort zones and habits that affect the more complex aspects of our lives, including how we communicate and relate with people.

Another value of this insight into the difficulty of getting rid of old ideas: As you begin to use Social Styles, one of the first challenges you will face is to catch yourself repeating habitual, relationship-inhibiting patterns in the ways you interact with people. Think back to the arm-crossing exercise we asked you to do in Chapter 2. You learned in that simple activity that there will be awkward moments when you begin to become aware of Social Style differences between yourself and others but are not always sure how to respond. These are the instances when habit can become a trap for you.

Here is why.

There are three basic steps that occur in most human interactions:

- We observe.
- We draw conclusions about what we see and hear.
- We respond to what we observe.

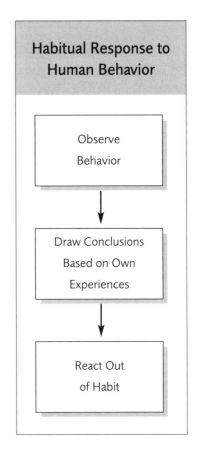

Habitual Response to Human Behavior

Observe Behavior

↓

Draw Conclusions Based on Own Experiences

↓

React Out of Habit

The cycle starts all over again when we observe the outcome of that response.

The problem is that most often we base our conclusions on the assumption that the other person is standing in *our* shoes, or at least shoes very much like ours. When we take that "typical" approach, we limit our understanding to projecting only from our own thoughts, experiences and feelings about similar situations. As a result, we may easily and frequently misinterpret what other people think and feel. (We'll talk more about thinking and feeling in the next chapter.)

Unfortunately this practice is very common. All too often our reactions to other people's behaviors are instinctively based on what we know would make *us* comfortable in a similar situation. *This is habit at its worst.*

At work, for example, this habitual response usually results in our treating each colleague in the same way. That approach lets us stay in our own comfort zone. This can be seductive, even if it's unproductive. As we noted before, three or more times out of four our comfort zones won't match those of other people, which can cause them varying degrees of discomfort. Imagine what would happen if you suddenly began to treat each colleague in a way that matches the way he or she likes to be treated?

ADAPTING – BETTER THAN JUST REACTING

A more productive pattern for effective communication is to focus on being versatile instead of habitual.

- Identify the other person's Social Style, taking into account what you will learn about Social Styles in this book.
- Reflect on the person's style, thinking about what makes people of this Social Style feel comfortable.
- Modify your own behaviors in ways that will create comfort for *the other person.*

The payoff? Research shows in the sales arena that there is a strong correlation between high Versatility – adapting instead of reacting – and high performance. It can be a bit more difficult to measure empirically the benefits of Versatility in other professions and situations, but accomplished Social Style practitioners across the board confirm that breaking old communication habits makes them better at what they do.

Ann Horner of Bourne Leisure Limited says, "I'm not sure I can specifically quantify the value of using what I know about Social Styles, but I know I wouldn't want to try to do my job without it."

STYLE MODIFICATION

In the end, you'll break your less effective communication habits by using what we call style modification.

You will see improvements in your Versatility and your relationships immediately with only small adaptations and modifications in your behaviors. For really significant results, however, you will want to learn and practice the

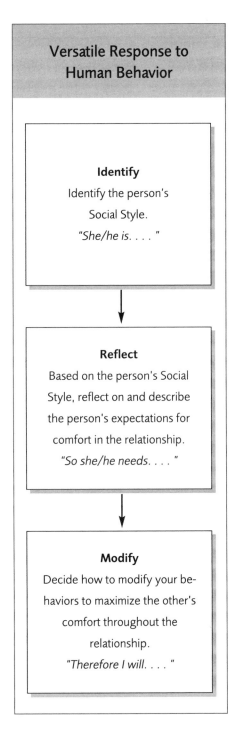

Versatile Response to Human Behavior

Identify
Identify the person's
Social Style.
"She/he is. . . . "

Reflect
Based on the person's Social
Style, reflect on and describe
the person's expectations for
comfort in the relationship.
"So she/he needs. . . . "

Modify
Decide how to modify your behaviors to maximize the other's
comfort throughout the
relationship.
"Therefore I will. . . . "

Social Style Modification Strategies

When you learn to identify others' Social Style, you can use this table to help you adapt your behavior to match their comfort zones. You can use the strategies that form the borders of another person's type to shape and modify your behavior.

ANALYTICAL

- Talk about the task; reference facts as well as feelings
- Try to organize your thoughts in a logical pattern when communicating
- Acknowledge the ideas and points that others make
- Articulate expected results of taking action

DRIVER

Increasing Task-Directed Responsiveness

- Be open to others' opinions, concerns and feelings
- Acknowledge the value you place on other people's time
- Demonstrate a willingness to follow the lead of others
- Ask for cooperation, but don't demand it

Increasing Ask-Directed Assertiveness

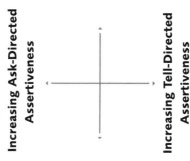

Increasing Tell-Directed Assertiveness

- Demonstrate a willingness to get to the point
- Volunteer information you have to others
- Be willing to express points of disagreement
- Summarize the positions you feel others are suggesting

Increasing People-Directed Responsiveness

AMIABLE

- Take the time to establish rapport with your co-workers
- Reinforce other people when they express good ideas
- Share your feelings or personal information
- Allow yourself and others to break the routine while problem solving

EXPRESSIVE

modification skills specifically suited for relating with each Social Style.

You have learned the basic challenges and opportunities in recognizing and changing your communication comfort zone and habits. Section 3, Social Styles In Depth, will provide many more details and plenty of lessons learned from the experiences of people using Social Styles regularly in their personal and professional lives.

SUMMARY

- New ideas come easy, but old habits die hard.
- In the "typical" pattern of communication, we make observations based on how we would react in certain situations and fail to take into account the communication style preferences others feel.
- The quickest way to improve communication is to adapt and modify our own behavior in response to observations we make about other people's Social Styles.
- Research shows that Versatility pays off in better performance. People who use Social Styles as a tool have trouble imagining doing their jobs without it.

9 Generalizing and Judging – Pros and Cons

Our mind is capable of passing beyond the dividing line we have drawn for it. Beyond
the pairs of opposites of which the world consists, other, new insights begin.
HERMANN HESSE

It may seem overly simple to categorize the planet's six billion people into only four Social Styles. We would agree with that assessment, *if* the Analytical, Driver, Expressive, and Amiable groupings were intended to generalize anything other than differences in communication behaviors. *They are not.*

Wilson Learning's nearly 40 years of research, with data on two million people, solidly demonstrates that by watching what people do and by listening carefully to what people say and how they say it, we can confidently identify individuals as belonging to one of these four styles. One of the great communication traps, however, is the natural inclination many of us have to try reading or interpreting other people's thoughts and feelings, and then letting those impressions – consciously or unconsciously – influence our own behaviors with them. It's hard to avoid this trap.

"Perception is reality." What we see is what we believe, even if in fact it isn't true. If we allow ourselves, for example, to interpret another person's brusqueness, loud voice, clipped phrases and stern-looking face as indicating a feeling of anger or irritation, we may be totally misreading the situation and responding inappropriately as a result.

Another person's thoughts and feelings will always be influential factors in a relationship, but the reality in most situations is that we can never really know the emotions or ideas going on inside someone else and influencing their conduct. Social Style focuses exclusively on words and actions – the everybody-can-see-and-hear elements of behavior. Social Style stays clear of trying to interpret the thinking and feelings behind those behaviors. In the example above, for instance, the behavioral signs all may merely indicate a preference by this person to take care of business as quickly, decisively, and matter-of-factly as possible.

Our inability to ever know with certainty what someone else is thinking or feeling is undeniable in professional situations like these. Social Style practitioners also find this true in almost all relationships, however, even with spouses, family members, and their closest friends, which is why using Social Styles can be a life-changing experience.

WHEN GENERALIZATIONS AND JUDGMENTS MAKE SENSE

There is always a risk in making generalizations about people. After all, broad statements and sweeping assessments tend to be associated with narrow-mindedness.

So why do we prescribe not only generalizing but also judging?

The intent of Social Style is to use generalizations and judgments to help you deepen, not flatten, your understanding of different people's behavior. Under the conditions we're describing – focusing on observable behaviors – generalizing about people's behavior can lead to an enriched understanding of them, and, of course, ourselves.

In most cases when people talk about being judgmental, there is an implication that the assessments made carry a positive or negative label, and probably invoke stereotypes that lead to misunderstandings about individual differences. The use of generalization and judgment in Social Style differs in two crucial ways. First, as we have said, the behavior being evaluated is tied to what is on the "outside" of the person (words, tone, and body language), not what's on the "inside" (thoughts, feelings, character or personality). Second, the conclusions we draw from Social Style concepts are research-based, independent of subjective opinion.

Using Social Styles will give you an objective way to understand the behavior of others and to adapt your own, in order to improve communication and enhance your relationships.

BEHAVIOR, FEELING, AND THINKING

The challenge is in generalizing and judging about *behavior*, and not doing so about thoughts and feelings. This is also greatly influenced by the comforts of habit discussed back in Chapter 8.

Ann Horner of Bourne Leisure Limited has been using Social Style for more than 20 years, but acknowledges she still sometimes falls into the trap of focusing on what people are thinking or feeling.

"The way I get out of it is to focus on positive intent. If I assume that people are trying to work for the same intent, if they are trying to work for the same answer as I am, I can remember to be more versatile in my own behavior.

"In any normal day I could be in a series of meetings with a variety of people to deal with everything from planning challenges to legal matters, marketing strategies, or personnel issues. There is no way I or anyone else can claim to be an expert in all of these things. So I have to surround myself with people who have different expertise and styles. Leadership roles change all the time in situations like this.

"For example, we have one brilliant manager who looks af-

Behavior and Feeling Defined

Behavior: An observable, measurable, externalized action; something you say or do.

Feeling: An internalized emotion that is not directly evident to observers; something you may or may not disclose through behavior.

ter our arcades in our resorts. He's always asking questions. I could say, 'What is he thinking? What's bothering him? Why does he ask so many questions?' I could challenge that behavior, but I have to stop and remind myself that his questioning has a way of helping us deliver great results.

"There are days when I think there are people who are more concerned about establishing their own importance than they are about the welfare of the company. . . when the intent is questionable. But we strive to create a no-blame culture. We spend a lot of time working together looking for solutions.

"If that's my focus, it helps me value people's differences. After all, why do I need help from someone else just like me to solve a problem I can't solve?"

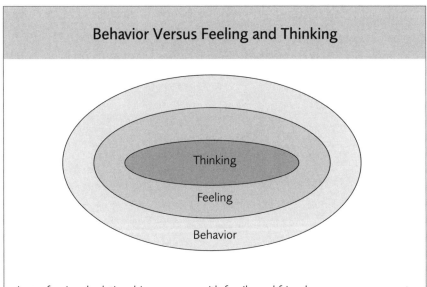

Behavior Versus Feeling and Thinking

Thinking

Feeling

Behavior

In professional relationships, or even with family and friends, you may never get close enough to understand what the other person is thinking or feeling, but you can always observe and adapt to the messages delivered by observable behavior.

SUMMARY

- Based on 40 years of research about *observable* human behavior, we can confidently divide natural behavior of people throughout the world into four Social Styles – Analyticals, Drivers, Expressives and Amiables.

- It's critical to use Social Styles based on what you see in other people's behaviors, not based on trying to guess at or interpret what they may be thinking or feeling.

- Generalizing and being judgmental about people is useful in the context of Social Style when the intent is to interpret predictable behavior patterns. This can help broaden, not limit, your understanding of people's communication and relationship preferences.

- Assuming positive intent is a good beginning to appreciating others' Social Style and contributions.

- Even experienced Social Style practitioners occasionally fall into the trap of trying to guess about other people's thoughts and feelings. Avoid that problem by focusing on your common intents and by remembering that diversity in Social Styles is an extremely valuable force.

10 | Back-Up Behavior – Fight or Flight

It is not necessary to change. Survival is not mandatory.

W. EDWARDS DEMING

Perhaps the reason you are reading *The Social Styles Handbook* is that you've had some important relationships become so strained they are on the verge of being damaged. You have reached the point where someone is saying to you, through actions if not words, "I can't take this anymore."

You're observing what we call "Back-Up Behavior."

This is the point when relationship tension becomes so intense that interpersonal connections begin to unravel; relationships become unproductive, untenable or worse; and when communication is most difficult.

FIGHT OR FLIGHT TENDENCIES

By the time you are experiencing Back-Up Behavior in a relationship, you are in pretty deep trouble. That other person is looking for a way out, either through *fight* or *flight*. Although the human race has come a long way in finding ways to react to stress, we're all still tied biophysically to these primitive instinctual responses for self-preservation. Danger appears, there's a rush of adrenaline, and we make an instantaneous decision about what we're going to do to protect ourselves – stay and do battle, or run away.

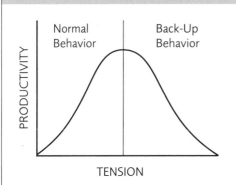

Tension and Back-Up Behavior

Normal Behavior | Back-Up Behavior

PRODUCTIVITY

TENSION

As we've seen before, the desirable increase in task tension can be very productive as you work with people. If relationship tension becomes too strong, however, Back-Up Behavior begins to diminish productivity.

You are at the point when you will need to be your versatile best.

When there is increasing relationship tension, most people tend to retreat deeper and deeper into their behavioral comfort zones. They begin to exhibit inflexible, less versatile versions of the behaviors normally associated with their Social Styles. As you might expect, people with the same Social Style tend to continue to behave in similar, predictable patterns when tension gets too high for comfort. People's Social Styles provide useful clues about what Back-Up Behaviors to expect, but fight or flight behaviors are not always revealed in obvious ways.

For example, the first sign of discomfort for people on the ask-directed end of the assertiveness scale – Analyticals and Amiables – is a tendency for flight. Because of the complexity of Back-Up Behavior, however, flight may not be nearly as obvious as someone literally walking away from you. Ask-directed people who have had enough of a relationship with you may show it in more subtle ways – avoiding you, not returning calls or e-mails, not having time to meet with you, etc. Despite any anger or deep frustration they might feel, you won't hear any shouting or see any table pounding as they separate from you. They will probably be much more subdued, and quietly withdraw.

An Amiable tends to acquiesce, giving in rather than fighting on principle ("Sure, do whatever you want."). An Analytical will withdraw through avoidance, not returning messages, putting a low priority on the task or relationship you share ("Sorry, haven't had time to figure out the details. Can we talk about this later?"). Both are fleeing, either from the task or relationship, but doing so quite differently.

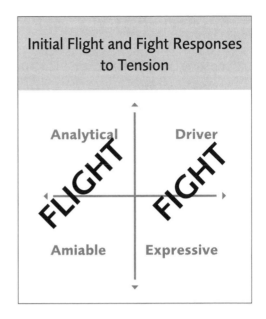

The tell-directed Drivers and Expressives tend at first to fight – challenging, bullying, and so on – as relationship tension gets extreme. They most often opt to stand their ground based on principles or positions.

A Driver will leave nothing uncertain ("Okay, let me tell you what you have to do to make this right: First, you will . . . "). An Expressive will make a point with emotional overtones ("I can't believe you're doing this to me! I'm holding you personally responsible."). Both are putting up hurdles that will make your relationship more difficult to maintain.

Back-Up Behavior is strictly defensive. It's aimed at self-protection, which makes it almost impossible to achieve your relationship goals.

There is good news about Back-Up Behavior in all four scenarios, however. Even relationships on the brink of disaster can be saved, if you read the signs as a warning – the earlier the better – and can muster the appropriate energy, ideas and commitment to treat the other person differently enough to restore comfort. Your chances of salvaging a failing relationship depend on your ability to move others back into a productive state of mind.

BACK-UP RECOVERY STRATEGIES – LSCPA

In general, the strategy for dealing with fight behaviors is to *neutralize* those aggressive behaviors. The strategy for dealing with flight behaviors is to *intervene*.

We'll discuss Back-Up Behaviors – and how to handle them – for each Social Style in detail in Section 3, Social Styles In Depth. There is one tool, however, you can use in relationships with people of all Social Styles whenever conflict causes Back-Up. It's called the LSCPA Model. We will introduce it here so you can have it mind as you learn more about each Social Style in the next chapters.

The LSCPA model is a process with five elements:

Listen

Share

Clarify

Problem-Solve

Ask for Action

LSCPA is an effective approach that is recommended by business people, mental health professionals, and others for dealing with conflict in business and personal situations. Since the applications of LSCPA really vary only slightly (but significantly) as you work with people of different Social Styles, you also may want to bookmark this section so you can refer to it in the context of the specific Social Styles we'll focus on later.

Listen

It is important to hear completely the concerns of a person in Back-Up. Pay attention for the facts, the beliefs and the feelings that are expressed when someone is frustrated with your relationship. Encourage people to talk openly about anything that is troubling them, and listen until there is nothing more to hear.

Pay attention to body language as you listen, and even after you listen. Look for clues in people's eyes and movements that will reveal their comfort or tension levels.

The true power of this kind of listening is your acknowledgment of the other person's concerns. Most likely, at this stage, people experiencing excessive relationship tension are not interested in hearing rational explanations for what has gone wrong; they just want you to know what's bothering them.

- Listen out of respect – not so you can dispute the facts of the situation.
- Don't interrupt.
- Stay calm.
- Use your own body language to demonstrate that you are attentive and encourage them to keep talking.

Share

Your goal in this stage is to make it clear to others you understand what they are saying and feeling. You may not agree with what you are hearing, but that doesn't matter. You need to empathize with their concerns and understand their perceptions of the situation without judging or, worse, debating.

The goal is to help ease people back to a state of calm; challenging them at this point is not a good way to soothe frayed emotions. Show your empathy by using phrases such as, "You're angry and I can understand why," and "You seem to feel strongly about that." Avoid arguing at all costs.

Clarify

In many cases, the concerns people first raise when feeling stressed will not be the real sources of their frustration. Listen and then restate what you hear to encourage people to help you fully understand what is happening. Ask questions to make sure you are truly identifying the root causes of their problems. For example, a customer or client may show anger with you about something that actually begins with a problem in his or her own organization. You may be surprised by a strong negative reaction to a new price schedule, for example, even though cost did not seem to be an issue as your negotiations progressed. Is expense truly the issue, or has an internal policy change or budget cut within your customer's organization created new barriers? You must find out.

- Restate the problems you hear in your own words and ask questions to verify you've understood the problem from the other person's point of view.
- Turn objections into questions. With an unhappy colleague, for example, move the conversation in this direction: "You say the deadline we agreed on won't work. Why exactly is that? Has something changed since we first discussed this time frame?"
- Ask as many questions as you need answered to understand all the facts and all the feelings at play in this stage of Back-Up. Some people may not understand what their problems are, or may not want to take any personal responsibility for those problems. This kind of questioning can help you and them pinpoint the challenges and difficulties.

Problem-Solve

Once you fully understand the problems, start thinking and talking again about new solutions for making your relationship productive and beneficial. If you are dealing with unhappy customers, assure them you have dealt with similar situations before and can handle theirs, too. If you are leading a team that has hit an impasse, make it clear you've overcome similar hurdles in the past. Then, put together a strategy that addresses the true concerns in a timely, satisfactory way.

Ask for Action

The final step in the LSCPA model is to get feedback about what you propose to people in response to their dissatisfaction, and then to ask for action. Ask if the concern has been addressed adequately. Agree on a solution. Make plans to follow through on what you have agreed upon for next steps.

Although LSCPA is laid out in what seems to be a logical, step-by-step sequence, the reality is you may have to cycle through some of the steps several times before you are able to restore a relationship to a comfortable tone.

It might also seem reasonable to expect you can accomplish all of these recovery goals in one conversation, but depending upon the complexity of the situation and the number of people involved in the relationship, it could take much longer.

ADAPTING LSCPA TO FIGHT OR FLIGHT BEHAVIOR

It is important to adapt the LSCPA model based upon an individual's fight or flight tendencies. The adaptation occurs primarily in the *Listen* and *Share* steps.

As we said earlier, for fight behaviors, the strategy is to *neutralize*. For flight behaviors, the strategy is to *intervene*.

To help neutralize the *Attacking* or *Autocratic* fight tendencies in relationships, let people vent by using the following techniques:

- Allow people to get their feelings out. Your goal is to get past their defensive fighting stance so you can identify the real problems that may be behind their anger.
- Accept their comments without judgment or automatic rebuttal.
- Listen to people's upset feelings, with your goal being to demonstrate you accept their differences with you and value their relationship with you.
- Don't interrupt and don't correct.
- Ask enough questions to get the venting started and finished.
- Stay attentive, relaxed, and non-confrontational.
- Once the issues are completely aired, *clarify* the core problem before moving back to problem-solving – the **C** step in LSCPA.

Back-Up Behaviors

ANALYTICAL – AVOIDING

- Avoids confrontation
- Draws attention away from an issue
- Retreats to other distractions
- Delays decisions

DRIVER – AUTOCRATIC

- Confronts others
- Focuses on the issue
- Looks for rationale
- Becomes demanding

AMIABLE – ACQUIESCING

- Smooths relationships
- Yields to others' viewpoints
- Wavers on opinion; hesitates
- Gives in; withdraws support

EXPRESSIVE – ATTACKING

- Confronts others
- Verbalizes judgmental feelings
- Blames others personally
- Shows extreme emotion

You will learn more about the Back-Up Behaviors of each Social Style in the next chapters, but this chart gives you the initial behaviors to expect in relationships when people are upset.

If you are dealing with a flight style of Back-Up, such as *Avoiding* or *Acquiescing* behaviors, then you can try to adapt LSCPA with a strategy to *intervene*. Your challenge is to draw out information and feeling from the person in Back-Up, using the following basic techniques:

- Get the issue on the table so it can be addressed rather than ignored.
- Ask questions to find out what is bothering the other person or people.
- Be persistent, but not pushy.
- Try to uncover the specifics of what has gone wrong. This may be difficult at first. Ask-directed people in flight often prefer to be vague and evasive.
- Show genuine concern.
- Acknowledge and confirm people's feelings. Assure them it is okay to disagree with you.
- Share your own feelings about the situation. This can help encourage more open disclosure of concerns on their parts.
- Once the issues are completely aired, *clarify* the core problem before moving back to the task of problem-solving – the **C** step in LSCPA.

How to Respond to Various Social Style Back-Up Behaviors

Social Style	Initial Backup Behavior	Your Response
Analytical	Flight	Intervene
Amiable	Flight	Intervene
Driver	Fight	Neutralize
Expressive	Fight	Neutralize

SUMMARY

- When a relationship is on the verge of being lost, you have reached the point where Back-Up Behavior begins.
- People exhibiting Back-Up Behavior are looking for a way out of your pressure by way of *fight* or *flight* – the instinctual response for self-preservation.
- The initial Back-Up Behavior for people on the ask-directed side of the assertiveness continuum is *flight*, often by way of Avoidance or Acquiescence.

- The initial Back-Up Behavior for people on the tell-directed side of the assertiveness continuum is *fight*, which often shows up as behaviors that are Attacking or Autocratic.
- There are two main strategies for dealing with Back-Up Behavior:
  1) Intervene with those in flight mode.
  2) Neutralize with those who are in the fight mode.
- The LSCPA model is useful tool for dealing with Back-Up Behavior with people of all Social Styles: **L**isten, **S**hare, **C**larify, **P**roblem-Solve, and **A**sk for **A**ction.
- You must adapt the LSCPA model in the Listen and Share stages based on whether the other person is fighting with you or fleeing from you. If people are fighting, let them vent. If they are fleeing, you must draw out their concerns.

11 | Building Relationships – Entry, Dialogue and Closure

To the man who only has a hammer in the toolkit, every problem looks like a nail.

ABRAHAM MASLOW

We compete for attention in every relationship in our lives, and the competition is intense.

We compete with the inestimable number of messages from the media, as well as the phone calls, e-mails and paper piles that inundate people daily. Then there is the world's seemingly insatiable appetite for meetings, and the swirling flow of co-workers, customers, business partners, solicitors, service providers, family members and the countless other people in the communities in which we interact. . . all contending for a few minutes of precious time.

The challenge is to be heard and respected through all that clamor. And it's especially important in the relationships that matter to us most. That's when it's most important to be heard and respected as quickly, completely – and comfortably – as possible.

Learning the Social Style concepts and applying Versatility will help deliver those positive results for you. Before you learn about each Social Style in detail, however, there are some essential tools, in addition to the LSCPA model covered in Chapter 10, that you should know about for improving your overall skills in listening to and communicating with others, regardless of Social Style.

In nearly forty years of working with, researching, and refining the use of Social Styles, Wilson Learning has developed many tools and concepts for organizing the process of relationship building. One of the most useful concepts is to think of relationships developing in three stages: Entry, Dialogue and Closure. Keep in mind as you read

Three Key Concepts for Productive Communication

While you may find it easier to remember these concepts if you learn them as stages, in practice you'll soon find yourself moving among them, as tasks, events and your relationship dictate.

Entry

- Create comfort to focus on the task
- Establish a trusting climate
- Identify a specific task
- Reduce relationship tension

Dialogue

- Identify needs and/or mutually solve problems
- Listen to learn
- Explore
- Integrate ideas
- Balance relationship and task tension

Closure

- Conclude with a clearly understood plan
- Agree on the resolution
- Implement your decisions
- Reaffirm the relationship
- Increase task tension

about each stage that this is not necessarily a sequential or linear model. Although you will see Entry is often the logical first phase in establishing an interpersonal connection, you may find it beneficial to move in and out of the different stages constantly as your relationships evolve.

ENTRY

Entry is the phase of a relationship in which you work on building trust, comfort, and creating a sense of credibility so you can begin to focus on tasks. If you haven't earned trust and credibility from another person, you really don't have a relationship that can be very productive. In this stage of building a connection with another person, you should be focused on reducing or eliminating relationship tension.

As you recall, high relationship tension depresses task tension and productivity drops as a result.

Purpose, Process and Payoff (PPP) Statements

One of the most important Entry tools in Wilson Learning's kit for easing relationship tension is the use of Purpose, Process and Payoff statements (called PPPs). They are especially useful when meeting a person or a group for the first time, but also at the start of subsequent discussions, meetings and documents. In the upcoming individual Social Style chapters, we'll include recommendations about how the content and delivery style of these statements should vary depending on the other person's Social Style and depending upon where you are in the process at the moment – Entry, Dialogue or Closure. The basics of these statements, however, will remain the same:

- *Purpose.* One of the first things you want to do when you initiate contact with someone is to clearly state why you are meeting – or calling on the phone, writing, etc. The Purpose statement lets people know the specific reason for your contact and what you hope to accomplish together.

- *Process.* Use the process statement to tell people what you are going to do while you are together and how.
- *Payoff.* Payoff statements tell people the benefits they'll all get from the time and energy they invest.

For example, if you convene a staff meeting to wrap up an ongoing strategic planning process, you might say,

- *(Purpose)* "I scheduled this meeting so we can finish planning for our year-end goals and objectives."
- *(Process)* "I would like to have each of us present the elements of the plan we agreed to prepare last week, then take 30 minutes to make sure we've considered how those pieces overlap and connect. Then let's use the remainder of the time scheduled to agree on the final combination and prioritization of the elements."
- *(Payoff)* "We'll walk out of this meeting room today with the plan complete and a clear picture of what we each need to accomplish before the end of the fiscal year. Does that sound like a good plan?"

Purpose, Process, Payoff statements can also work in more personal situations – with a forgetful, disorganized neighbor who likes to borrow things, for example.

- *(Purpose)* "Hello, Etienne, I stopped by to pick up my hedge trimmer that you borrowed last month."
- *(Process)* "I can see you're busy cutting your grass with my lawn mower that you borrowed from my garage this morning, so I'll just go into your garage and hunt through the piles. I'm sure my trimmer is in there somewhere. Don't worry, you keep working and I'll let you know if I need help."
- *(Payoff)* "If I find it quickly, I'll be able to get my bushes trimmed by the time you finish mowing and return my mower, and then I can cut my grass, too. Is that all right with you?"

Credibility

It's also important in the Entry stage to be aware of the impression you make with people about your credibility. We have identified four critical components to credibility:

- *Propriety.* Based on the circumstances of where and why you are interacting with someone, do you meet that person's expectations about appropriate customs and behaviors? This takes into account everything from how you dress to how you speak.

Versatility for Entry	
Versatility skills: Modify your behavior in these ways, with respect to the Social Style of the other person, to increase comfort.	**Warning Signs of Discomfort:** Watch for these signs of discomfort in a relationship when you are in the Entry stage.
Establish a comfortable climate • Open interactions in a way that makes the other person comfortable • Show sensitivity to time and work priorities to others • Confirm you are intent on having a win-win relationship **Identify a specific task** • Come to discussions or meeting prepared • Provide a clear purpose for a meeting or discussion • Discuss a process or agenda to follow	• Resistance • Distraction • Insistence • Argumentativeness

- *Competence.* Do you exhibit the ability, background, skills, talent, and experience to make this other person confident about the prospects of developing a beneficial relationship with you?
- *Commonality.* Is there evidence that you share areas of mutual interest, values or experience?
- *Intent.* Trust is essential in Entry. Are you making it clear by what you say and how you behave that your motives in building a relationship with this person are based on mutual interest, not just your own self-interest?

DIALOGUE

During this stage of relationship building your task is to get to know the other person's needs and interests, and for them to get to know yours. Your objective is to develop a mutual understanding of the situation you share and establish what might be helpful in moving the relationship to the next level of comfort, on the way to achieving mutual goals.

The most important parts of Dialogue are effective listening, exploring and integration skills. We'll take up each of these in turn.

Listening

Listening is critical to effective Dialogue. Only by actively listening to others do you develop a good sense of their opinions, priorities, and needs. But listening is more than just having your ears open; it is actively encouraging others to express themselves, and continuously checking to make sure you understand them. We have identified three important techniques that contribute to effective listening during the Dialogue stage:

- *Responsive Listening,* which includes using verbal and nonverbal behavior and signals to reinforce what the other person is saying and to make it clear you are listening attentively. Nodding, taking notes, saying "I see," or making other reinforcing sounds are some of these signals.

- *Restatement*, which is a process for paraphrasing what the other person says in order to summarize what you hear and to verify that you have understood correctly. "In other words, you're saying. . . "
- *Checking*, which is a method similar to *Restatement* but focused on making sure you have an accurate understanding of the other person's situation. "Did you say you have 21 days to complete this project?"

Exploring

Listening alone, however, does not make for effective Dialogue. You need to explore the details and emotions attached to the other person's ideas or opinions, and express your own ideas in a way that invites an open and honest reaction to those ideas. Key to effective exploring is the use of questions. Questions serve two purposes: First, they allow you to get deeper into the other person's ideas, and second, they allow you to express yourself in a way that will not be considered threatening. There are several classifications of questions that can be used in Exploring during a Dialogue. Let's look at a few:

- *Permission Questions.* It is good to ask this type of question before stating an opinion, presenting options, and especially before asking clarifying questions. In a job-hiring situation, for example, you might say, "We have several openings that seem to fit the experience you described in your résumé. Is it okay if I ask you a few questions first to make sure I'm clear about the specifics of what you've done in the past?" Or, in a customer service situation, you might say, "I can think of two ways we might resolve your current problem. Do you mind if I describe these to you to get your opinion on which is the best approach?"
- *Fact-Finding Questions.* Use these when you need to gather facts and data, or to test someone's reaction to your facts. In a budget planning situation, for example: "What kind of DVD replication equipment are you using now? How many units does it produce in a

day?" Or, to express your facts: "Our equipment has an average up-time of 98.5 percent when we schedule two hours of down-time each month for routine maintenance. What is your current equipment's down-time?"

- *Feeling-Finding Questions.* These will help you understand another person's opinions, feelings, values, and beliefs – and allow you to express your opinions without fear of cutting off the conversation. They are especially powerful when used in combination with fact-finding questions. In a situation with an unhappy internal client or a business-to-business customer: "I know you are upset about the failure rate in this shipment of replacement parts, but how do you feel about the overall reliability and effectiveness of the rest of the products we've been providing this year?" Or, to express a feeling or belief: "Our organization feels that our attention to customer service is one of our strengths, and we put considerable effort into maintaining high customer satisfaction. How do you feel about the level of service you have been receiving from us? Does it match your expectations of us?"

- *Best-Least Questions.* "What do you like best about the leadership practices in our organization? What do you like least?"

- *Magic-Wand Questions.* Getting people dreaming a little, and allowing you both to dream together, can move a dialogue forward rapidly. "If you could wave a magic wand and make this team function at the highest possible level, what would we have to change about the way we work together?" Or "I often think about what it would take to create a world-class e-commerce system because it would really impact our long-term revenue. Have you thought about that? What do you think?"

Integrating

Dialogue will nearly always lead to the need to integrate everyone's ideas, opinions, priorities and values. Not all interactions require a formal action plan or agreement, but in business, the purpose of an interaction often means that some agreement or decision is reached or produced. Integration ensures that the agreement or decision is clearly expressed and that everyone involved understands and accepts it as part of the interaction.

- "So, if I understand it correctly, you need to move delivery up by one week. As we have discussed, this will require additional cost and effort on our part that was not included in the original contact. So, any solution we agree on will need to meet this new delivery date and address the additional expenses involved to expedite delivery. Is that your understanding?"

Versatility Skills for Dialogue

Versatility Skills:	Warning Signs of Discomfort:
Modify your behavior in these ways, with respect to the Social Style of the other person, to increase comfort.	Watch for these signs of discomfort in a relationship when you are in the Dialogue stage.

Listen to learn	• Silence
• Seek different points of view	• Defensiveness
• Check for accurate interpretation	• Lack of eye contact
Explore	• Inactive listening
• Offer ideas and opinions for discussion	• Closed body language
• Invite questions to test assumptions	• Rising voice
Integrate ideas	• Repeating information (indicating a sense of not being heard)
• Articulate the problem	• Attempting to close prematurely
• Consider multiple options	
• Combine ideas into innovative solutions	

- "Let me summarize: We all agree that the features in our first list are the most critical to develop into this revision of the product. However, we disagree about how critical the features in the second list are. So, in this meeting today we have agreed to go ahead with development of the first list, and will jointly conduct some client input sessions so we can better prioritize the second list. Is that an accurate summary?"

CLOSURE

It is during the Closure stage of relationship building that you focus on creating an agreed-upon plan, aligning people in the group or team with your point of view and goals for a relationship, and on influencing their thoughts, actions, and decisions. It helps to think in terms of:

- affirming the agreement,
- supporting the decision, and
- enhancing the relationship you've developed with the person in question.

One of the key points to recognize here is that you need to believe completely in what you bring to a relationship. Alignment between your interests and the interest of others can happen naturally if people trust you – thanks to your success in Entry – and you clearly understand what is important to them – because of what you accomplished while in Dialogue. Those two steps are critical to putting you in position to build a solid relationship, but Closure skills are essential to finishing the job. Regardless of how comfortable people feel with you or how sure you are that you understand their unique needs and interests, you won't make lasting personal or professional relationships if *they* don't see a compelling value in being involved with you. Closure confirms that you are making Progress on the relationship and task.

Affirming the agreement

This might sound a little legalistic, but stop and think how often you've agreed to do something relatively simple with someone and only in the course of time realized there was a misunderstanding. One easy technique to both clarify what everybody must do and secure alignment involves these three steps:

- *Define the solution*: "So we've agreed that we'll all meet at the hotel to run through our presentation at seven tomorrow morning in the meeting room, and Angelique will run the projection equipment."
- *Explain why it's a good solution*: "That way we can make sure our timing is tight and finalize who speaks when. Plus we'll be in place when the clients arrive at nine."
- *Show the benefits*: "I know after the run-through we'll all be much more relaxed and confident. That way we can concentrate on the client's reactions and be prepared for concerns and questions."

In a more informal setting, you might say, "Okay, so we'll all go to dinner at the Italian restaurant, leaving here in about 30 minutes. *(Defining the solution.)* That will give me time to finish what I am working on, but we'll still get to dinner early so we don't have to wait for a table. *(Explaining why it's a good solution.)* Does this sound alright with everyone?" *(Showing the benefits.)*

Supporting the decision

In all relationships, new or old, things happen that cause uncertainty and anxiety – those times when relationship tension increases to uncomfortable levels and trust and confidence may be shaken. Co-workers, colleagues, customers, and even close friends all need periodic evidence of your support, a sense that you will be there when they need you most. This often is necessary when a decision has been taken.

There are two things you can do in the Closure stage of building relationships that can help convey this sense of reliability and stability:

1. *Support Decisions.* "Buyer's remorse" is a phrase that can apply to just about everything from purchasing a home to deciding to vote for a specific person as the new managing partner of your firm. It can occur as last-minute uncertainty just before the actual decision, or much sooner in the decision-making process. It is a feeling that can also happen right after the decision and persist for quite a while. It's natural to feel some doubt about important decisions, but it can be stifling to let doubt become excessive. Your purpose is to keep people feeling positive about their decisions in order to keep things moving forward on the activities that are the focus of your relationship.

2. *Manage Plans.* Relationships inherently involve agreements and plans. Co-workers who have agreed under your leadership to complete their pieces of your department's strategic plan will want to know you are managing the flow of all the pieces and co-ordinating everybody else's deadlines. In a sales situation, after the checks are signed you may hand off your customer to others in your organization to handle the installation of the products you've sold. This can be a nervous time for the customer, so it's important for you to orchestrate a seamless transition that's de-signed to assure satisfaction.

Enhancing the relationship

Don't take important relationships for granted. Look for ways to make them better, to tap deeper into the potential you and others bring to them. There's a universal belief that it's almost always easier to earn new business from an existing satisfied customer, for example, than it is to sell to new customers. The obvious benefit to a salesperson is that when things go well with one sale it provides a great opportunity for exploring additional potential sales with the customer's company. The same is true with any relationship. Whatever defines success in a particular relationship for you, when things are going well the potential exists to enrich that relationship further.

Versatility Skills for Closure

Versatility Skills: Modify your behavior in these ways, with respect to the Social Style of the other person, to increase comfort.	Warning Signs of Discomfort: Watch for these signs of discomfort in a relationship when you are in the Closure stage.
Agree on the resolution • Confirm understanding and agreement of the decision **Implement the decision** • Clarify expectations about roles and responsibilities • Decide on next steps and take action **Reaffirm the relationship** • State the value of working together	• Silence • Closed body language • Delay in reaching agreement • Physical removal • Vagueness • Resistance • Delay in implementing a plan or agreement

Nonetheless, troubles occur in relationships, often as a result of things totally outside your control, or even because of the other person. Don't look for blame, even if it's clear you are not at fault. Look for resolution. Finger pointing is one of the quickest ways to undermine a relationship. Among other things, it will erode trust, which often takes longer to earn back than it takes to earn in the first place.

The upcoming chapters on living and working with people of specific Social Styles will provide additional Closure ideas that will help you find the shortest, straightest and most persuasive paths to helping people believe in you.

BUILDING TRUST

All the tools we've described in this chapter are designed to help you earn trust from people. There is nothing more important in the evolution of a relationship. Keep these trust-building pointers in mind as you use all these tools:

- Be open to other people and their ideas.
- Listen carefully to people's full messages before responding.
- Treat each person as unique and special. Be respectful.
- Don't try to "become" a different person or Social Style. Small behavior adjustments can demonstrate your willingness to be versatile in a relationship without compromising your personal integrity.
- Articulate and demonstrate a positive intent toward other people.
- Follow through on what you promise.

SUMMARY

If things go extremely well in relationships, you may begin to see people emulate your Versatility. Even without knowing anything specific about Social Styles, the important people in your life may begin to respond to your efforts to be more collaborative by increasing their own willingness to do the same. It's called reciprocity.

There's no guarantee that being versatile with others will make them versatile with you, but everything we've described so far is an outline for what it takes to make it possible for that to happen. When it does – when people recognize your honest efforts to respond to their needs and expectations – a special thing happens. Other people start making an effort to make you comfortable, too.

The energy and productivity that can come out of these kinds of situations is astounding. Somehow your common ground becomes bigger and you begin to focus your efforts on shared goals and outcomes. You have commitments to mutually beneficial causes.

- One of the biggest challenges in building relationships is to be heard and respected quickly through all the communication clamor in people's lives. That includes face-to-face talk, e-mails, reports, presentations and documents that come your way daily.

- Wilson Learning's Entry/Dialogue/Closure concept is an effective way to view the critical junctures in the development of any relationship.
- Relating means building trust and creating a sense of credibility.
- One of the most important *Entry* tools in Wilson Learning's kit for easing relationship tension is the use of Purpose, Process and Pay-off statements, which define the reason for meeting or communicating, how the meeting will be conducted or the communication will be structured, and the benefits for those involved.
- It's also important in the *Entry* stage to be aware of the impression you make with people in four critical areas: Propriety, Competence, Commonality and Intent.
- During the *Dialogue* stage of relationship building, your challenge is to get to know the other person's needs and interests.
- There are five categories of questions helpful in improving communication: Permission Questions, Fact-Finding Questions, Feeling-Finding Questions, Best-Least Questions and Magic-Wand Questions.
- *Closure* is concerned with aligning your mutual goals and interests so people feel compelled to act in your interest.
- Four things you can do to convey your reliability in a relationship are to support decisions, manage plans, deal with dissatisfaction, enhance the relationship.
- Trust, the foundation for open communication and productive relationships, is strongly related to your own personal integrity and positive intent. Knowing how other people's Social Style influence how they like to be treated opens the door to greater trust.

12 | The Social Style Self-Profiler

I could give you no advice but this: to go into yourself
and to explore the depths where your life wells forth.
RAINER MARIA RILKE

Throughout your reading of *The Social Styles Handbook* so far you have no doubt seen bits and pieces of yourself in the descriptions of each of the four Social Styles – Analytical, Driver, Amiable and Expressive. And you have been wondering, "What am I?"

This Social Style Self-Profiler tool will help you begin to pull together your thoughts and observations about where you and others you know fit in the Social Style matrix. The forty years' worth of data Wilson Learning has compiled about Social Styles is based on assessment instruments used in workshops that are considerably more scientific than what we can provide here.

Although this Self-Profiler tool cannot be as accurate, precise, or reliable as our assessment instruments, it can give you a starting place to understand your own style, and the styles of others around you.

It will be helpful for you to practice with this tool before heading into the chapters that go into greater detail about living and working in productive relationships with people of all four Social Styles. The tool provides a quick but inclusive overview that will prepare you for learning in-depth about the traits and behaviors for Analyticals, Drivers, Amiables and Expressives.

It will also be beneficial, however, to turn back to these pages after you have read the book completely.

To complete this Self-Profiler, follow these instructions:

1. First practice profiling others. Identify two or three people you know as examples of each of the four Social Styles.
2. Then, show these lists of characteristics to three to five other people you know and ask if they agree with your examples, and in which quadrant they would put you.
3. If at least three of the five people place you in the same quadrant, chances are that is your Social Style. If fewer than three people place you in the same quadrant, ask some additional people until you feel comfortable that there is a consensus.
4. If you can't get a consensus on your style, see if there are other patterns that will help you. For example, do most people see you as tell-directed (Driver and Expressive) or do most people see you as ask-directed (Analytical and Amiable)? This way you should be able to at least identify one clear dimension of your Social Style.

SOCIAL STYLE SELF-PROFILER

People to whom this
description applies:

_____

_____

_____

_____

_____

ANALYTICAL

Detail-oriented. Deliberate. Well-organized. Listens and studies information carefully before weighing all alternatives. Lets others take the social initiative. Prefers an efficient, businesslike approach. Prefers information presented in systematic manner. Conservative and practical in business decisions. Relies on structural approach and factual evidence. Reserved. Few gestures. Proper speech. Formal posture and appearance. Deliberate rate of speech.

People to whom this
description applies:

_____

_____

_____

_____

_____

AMIABLE

Warm. Cooperative. Attentive. Generally gathers information and processes it with others before making decisions. Wants to establish strong, trusting relationships. Wants decisions supported by others. Careful but cooperative. People-oriented. Relies on others. Prefers interactive problem solving. Friendly and open. Relaxed posture. Slow speech. Pleasant and soft voice. Open and eager facial expressions.

DRIVER

Forceful. Results-oriented. Controlled. Clear objectives. Focuses on results rather than relationships. High sense of urgency. Knowledgeable and forceful in business decisions. Goal-oriented. Relies on information that supports results. Acts quickly and confronts issues directly. Expects people to listen carefully and respond in a timely manner. Serious. Formal posture. Restrained gestures. Rapid speech. Direct. Voice inflection varies little, usually only to emphasize important points.

People to whom this description applies:

_____

_____

_____

_____

_____

EXPRESSIVE

Fast-paced. Outgoing. Enthusiastic. Tends to be guided more by vision that by facts. Establishes open, trusting relationships. Collaborates in finding and implementing quality solutions. Sees the big picture before probing for details. Futuristic. Holistic thinker. Inspiring. Direct and open. Energetic. Gestures that are open and wide. Voice that is loud and varied. Lively.

People to whom this description applies:

_____

_____

_____

_____

_____

SOCIAL STYLES IN DEPTH

| 13 | Living and Working with Analyticals |

An investment in knowledge pays the best interest.

BENJAMIN FRANKLIN

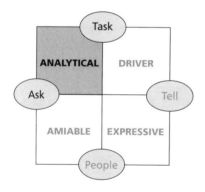

The four labels in the Social Style matrix provide strong and immediate clues about what to expect from people who fit each category. Intuition and instinct will go a long way in helping you use this tool to improve your communication and relationship skills.

The word "analytical," for example, implies an affinity for facts, figures, logic, reason, calm calculation, and careful assessment. Analyticals are the people who are ask-directed and task-directed on the assertiveness and responsiveness scales described in Chapter 4, and who land in the upper left quadrant of the Social Style matrix. Analyticals typically approach the world asking questions and staying on task. They want to examine as much information as possible before moving ahead with relationships or projects, and they typically do so using logical, orderly processes.

As Ann Horner of Bourne Leisure Limited says, "Analyticals always seem to know the right questions to ask."

Analyticals are often perceived as deliberate, thorough, and inclined to follow policies, procedures, rules, guidelines, regulations – even recipes – quite faithfully. They weigh all the alternatives in any situation and are usually steadfast in doing whatever needs to be done. They tend to be conservative, businesslike and persistent in their relationships.

Analyticals are most likely to invest in a relationship or pursue goals only after they have eliminated as much risk as possible and have compiled plenty of data to support the purpose and practicality of what they are about to undertake.

When you hear people describe them, they often say Analyticals:

- Seek structure, certainty and evidence before they make decisions.
- Appear quiet and unassuming and usually don't show much emotion when dealing with others.
- Are not likely to initiate social connections with people they don't know, and are not likely to share a lot of personal information until trust and confidence are built.
- Like to see how far they can keep going with existing relationships and ideas before they're ready to try something new.

ANALYTICAL EXPECTATIONS

In general, Analyticals prefer it when their world moves relatively slowly, precisely, and predictably.

One of the most important people in Sherry Schoolcraft's life is an Analytical – her youngest son, Scott. She teaches Social Style workshops for Wilson Learning, so she knows two critical facts about relationships with Analyticals, whether it's dealing with them on the personal or professional levels. First, she is an Expressive, which means an Analytical is diagonally opposite her in the Social Style matrix. With no commonality on either the assertiveness or responsiveness continua, Analyticals represent Expressives' greatest communication challenge. Second, she knows she must approach a relationship with someone in this quadrant strategically.

"If I want to make plans with Scott, I know I have to call ahead and get on his calendar. I can't think about getting together on the spur of the moment. There just isn't much spontaneity there.

"My oldest son, Sean, is an Expressive. I can be far more spontaneous with him, but it's much tougher to plan anything ahead. And when he and I do make plans, they can change at any moment."

Analyticals also make it clear through their behavior that they prefer building relationships in a relatively reserved manner. Passion – whether it is about a person, a project, or a product for sale – is often at the heart of strong and productive relationships. But Analyticals express their passion differently from other styles. Rather than say or show with body language how passionate they are, they are more likely to express it by giving the task all of their attention, working longer and harder at something than normal. Therefore, with Analyticals, expressing too much passion, or too much passion too soon, isn't usually what they are looking for. In a work relationship, for example, if you act too tell-assertive or even too personal with Analyticals too quickly, you run the risk of coming across as unprofessional.

That, of course, is one of the quickest ways to make an Analytical uncomfortable and create relationship tension. Overt enthusiasm doesn't sit well with them. You'll be more likely to reduce relationship tension with an Analytical by initially being moderately cordial, but not chummy, especially in relatively new professional relationships. In all scenarios with Analyticals, it also helps to be diligently prepared to deal with the task at hand.

Somebody in Sherry's situation, for example, probably shouldn't consider calling an Analytical son to make dinner plans without first

The Analytical Social Style

Detail-oriented. Deliberate. Well-organized. Listens to and studies information carefully before weighing all alternatives. Lets others take the social initiative. Prefers an efficient, businesslike approach. Prefers information presented in systematic manner. Conservative and practical in business decisions. Technically oriented. Relies on structural approach and factual evidence.

Verbal and Nonverbal Cues	Reserved. Few gestures. Proper speech. Formal posture and appearance. Listens well. Deliberate rate of speech.
Work Style	Fairly independent. Follows structured approaches.
Attitude about Time	"Take time to deal with matters objectively and logically. Move with deliberation."
Attitude about Accomplishment	"The process used for getting results is almost as important as the results themselves."
Attitude about Others	"Relationships take time to develop, and someone else will probably make the initial effort to make a new contact."
Natural Work Activity Strengths	Planning and organizing.
Personal Motivator	Respect: Seeks to enhance reputation as a technical expert by making the right decision in the right way. Values being recognized for accomplishments and respected for expertise.
Common Misperceptions about Analyticals	No feelings and no ability to have fun.

reviewing her own calendar, selecting a couple of optional dates and times, pre-selecting choices for a restaurant, and maybe even having contingency plans just in case the weather is too bad for driving or one of the grandchildren becomes ill. In a work situation or on a sales call that involves Analyticals, come prepared to deliver a businesslike presentation based on well-organized, well-researched, expert-driven data.

If your supervisor is an Analytical, you will notice she often seems uncomfortable or impatient in conversations about holiday travels or children's teams or hobbies, and prefers to focus instead on the work you must do together. Your relationship with an Analytical might evolve to the point where "small talk" eventually may be well received or even desired, but it is not where they will most often seem most comfortable. In most instances with Analyticals, whose behaviors fall into this ask-directed task-directed quadrant of the Social Style matrix, it pays to get to the point, but then allow them time to process the message.

Analyticals expect you to:

- *Adopt a predictable, task-oriented approach with them.* They are naturally most comfortable when they can operate with a high degree of objectivity.
- *Be well prepared.* Get the details right. If you are managing a project with or for Analyticals, double-check every fact, every number. If you are making a sales presentation to an Analytical customer, know the name and title of every person present, and be well versed with as much background information as possible. Errors in grasping these kinds of details can seriously damage your credibility with Analyticals.
- *Be focused.* Carefully organize your work to make sure it is entirely pertinent to the task or problem that is the focus of your relationship with Analyticals. They don't want *all the data*, they just want *all the relevant data.*

- *Be deliberate but flexible.* Analyticals like to see a relationship move along at a deliberate pace, but they also want sufficient time for thoughtful consideration of the key issues being explored in your project or points of contact.
- *Offer quick confirmation of the expertise you bring to the relationship.* Analyticals want to feel confident you can provide factual information worth weighing.
- *Document and be detailed.* When you think you have provided all the information there is, some Analyticals will be just warming up to ask for more. Usually, delivering data effectively is the only kind of interpersonal assurance Analyticals require. Respect is their measure of personal value – respect for authentic data and for expertise.
- *Support their principles and reasoning.* By the time you meet with Analyticals in a professional situation, they will have done much work and preparation related to the challenges and issues central to your relationship. When you present ideas and proposals to Analyticals, be certain your view of the situation is consistent with the way they see things. It comforts Analyticals to deal with people they know will follow step-by-step, predictable processes as they work together.
- *Furnish solid evidence to help them make up their minds.* Analyticals want you to provide as much relevant, accurate data as they need to feel they are making completely informed decisions. It also helps to put critical and influential data into writing for Analyticals.

ENTRY WITH ANALYTICALS

One of the main obstacles to communicating and building great relationships is the failure to create a sense of trust, comfort and confidence. As we described in Chapter 11 when we introduced the Entry/Dialogue/Closure model developed by Wilson Learning, it is important to create comfort and establish credibility early on in a relationship. What many people often misunderstand is that dealing with this challenge early on does not mean it happens quickly. Building trust, comfort and confidence takes time. It is vital to slow down and proceed consciously. Take a moment to remind yourself about what Analyticals value and expect in the context of the current situation. Then make a deliberate effort to relate to them in the ways in which they feel most comfortable. Use Versatility.

In the Entry stage with Analyticals, that means it can be helpful to:

- Research their situation and needs as thoroughly as possible before you meet, and be prepared to demonstrate your knowledge, background, skill and special talents. If you are assigned to work on a special project with a manager you don't know personally, talk to others who do. If you are interviewing for a position with a new company, search for articles on the Internet about the organization. Visit the company's Web site. Look for items in the local newspaper. Talk to colleagues, friends, associates in professional organizations who might know anything about the industry sector, company or the individuals with whom you will interview. In these or other situations with Analyticals, use whatever information is available to help you get ready to show how and why you are the right person for the relationship.
- Use a Purpose, Process, Payoff statement to start. It is not something that is "nice to do" – with Analyticals, it is a "must do," with extra effort paid to the Process part. And, if it is a long discussion, then it might be wise to put a time frame on each step in the process (for example "First each of us will take 10 minutes to present our views, then we'll take one hour discussing the similarities and difference in our views. We can end the meeting by developing the action plan, perhaps taking 30 minutes."
- Double check and clarify logistical details. If you are planning meetings with Analyticals, ask and confirm the time and location. They appreciate the thoroughness.
- Don't open your conversations with small talk and self-disclosure.
- Slow down. In encounters with Analyticals, you should be prepared to provide a lot of information, but don't rush the flow of

data. Make certain you allow time for pauses, reflection and questions. When you ask a question and don't get an immediate answer, try not to speak just to fill the silence, even though you may feel uncomfortable. Wait. Analyticals often feel most comfortable making carefully considered replies or asking clarifying questions. Their pace is thoughtful and rhythmic.

- Ask Analyticals about their concerns, and then listen (as difficult as it may be), without interrupting.
- Anticipate the questions you may need to answer. Provide time for questions to clarify why you are together and what to expect from the time together. And focus on the results of what you are working on together. Prove you have done your homework about this person, but be very conscious of time.

Establishing your credibility (as described in Chapter 11) with Analyticals will also be different from how you establish it with the other styles:

- *Propriety:* Even in a casual work environment, Analyticals will expect fairly formal behavior and appearance. Being slightly more conservative than the situation calls for might be the best approach for a first meeting
- *Competence:* Show your competence by referencing specific factual data and experiences. While testimonials from others can be valuable to an Analytical, don't make them the major method for communicating your competence.
- *Commonality.* Focus on commonalities related to a task. While other styles may find it valuable that you both play golf, unless the task is to design a golf course, it will have little impact on the Analytical.
- *Intent.* Express your intent for the relationship in a factual and balanced way. Everyone naturally has self-interests at stake in an interaction. Analyticals will expect to hear both what is in it for them, and what is in it for you.

DIALOGUE WITH ANALYTICALS

The Dialogue phase is perhaps the most critical step in establishing a new relationship or maintaining an ongoing one in top shape. It's when you learn about what matters to the other person, and when you identify needs and begin to solve problems together. This is when you begin to establish your compatibility and to understand what it will take to communicate a sense of connection.

In the Dialogue stage of relationship building with Analyticals:

- Begin by asking specific fact-finding questions. Only later should you turn to more feeling-finding questions.
- Proceed in an organized and systematic manner.
- Listen to and note the details of your conversation, even if you're hearing more than you want to know.
- Set a slow, thoughtful, unhurried pace.
- Be thorough, but not redundant. The last thing you want an Analytical to think is that he or she is answering the same question more than once.
- Let Analyticals know when you are aligned with their thinking and can support their points of view.
- Encourage some discussion of ideas and feelings to provide balance to the factual information Analyticals prefer, but orient that discussion to the tasks or problems you are addressing.

Keep in mind that you are striving for a comprehensive exchange of information in this stage. Diligence in Dialogue pays off when you need to prove your grasp of a situation in order to influence an Analytical's thinking about issues critical to your relationship. Knowing the details makes it easier to make progress, and to handle objections, reservations or interpersonal problems. Remember to refer back to Chapter 11 for specific recommendations on questioning and listening skills that will help in the Dialogue stage – permission questions, fact-finding questions, feeling-finding questions, best-least questions, and magic-wand questions, as well as responsive listening, restatement, and checking techniques. Don't forget that body language plays a role, too.

When you are expressing your ideas, plans, and opinions with Analyticals,

- Try to state your opinions in the form of a question, not a directive (e.g., "My opinion is X – what do you think?" or "Do you think it would work if X?" or "Perhaps we could try X. What do you think?")
- Support your ideas and opinions with supportive facts.
- If an idea or opinion is complex, provide some details. Don't just state the "What," but also some of the "How" of the idea.

CLOSURE WITH ANALYTICALS

As noted earlier, in every relationship in our lives we are competing for attention and time. To help earn your share of those precious commodities with Analyticals so that you can develop a clearly understood plan, consider these options, related to the principles of affirming, supporting and enhancing the relationship.

Affirming

- Put whatever you can in writing, but whenever possible present that information in person. If you can't meet face to face, consider sending the information via fax or e-mail, then follow up with a phone call. In some business situations a teleconference or webcast might be good alternatives to meeting in person.
- Recommend specific courses of action.
- Clearly present all of your assumptions pertinent to the relationship or the task you are undertaking and how you arrived at them.
- Present your ideas, opinions and options in an organized, systematic and precise way.

Supporting

- If there are costs involved with your proposed course of action, include the strongest possible justification for the investment. This is appropriate whether you are recommending a stock purchase, hiring the job candidate who will require higher compensation, or choosing the more expensive restaurant for a dinner meeting.

- Be reserved but not cold, decisive but not aggressive.

- Limit your use of emotional appeals.

- Limit your use of references to "others who are doing it" as a rationale for why a recommended path should be followed.

- Provide an opportunity for a thorough review of all the data and documents related to a decision that must be made.

- Ask directly for what you need out of the relationship, but try to be low-key.

- Expect to negotiate changes in the details of whatever you propose with Analyticals and be ready to customize whatever final agreements you reach.

- Pay special attention to cost issues.

- Provide detailed plans, in writing when appropriate, that describe the behaviors and commitments at the core of the relationship.

- Clarify all roles, responsibilities and expectations about the relationship.

- Coordinate the distribution and use of resources you must share or otherwise manage in the relationship.

- Provide direct contact with any technical experts or other advisors influencing elements of the relationship. If you are overseeing implementation of a new computer system for your work team, for example, bring in the information technology folks doing the work to answer Analytical team members' questions about the installation and its impact.

- Limit the frequency of your follow-up. Analyticals want assurance and plenty of information, but there is a fine line between being thoroughly supportive and bothersome.

Enhancing

- If you are unable to answer an Analytical's specific question, offer to find the answer and come back with the information. Don't improvise or bluff.
- Provide accurate, periodic reviews about important developments.
- When you do follow-up, always bring some value-added information, either about the project you are working on together, or some research you have done into a topic you have a mutual interest in.
- Provide summaries related to costs and benefits of your mutual investments. Whether you are justifying a major product purchase to your firm's chief financial officer or planning with a spouse about saving for a child's college education, Analyticals want to be able to stay informed about the numbers.

When you reach those moments of doubt and concern with Analyticals – those times when relationship tension increases to uncomfortable levels and trust and confidence may be shaken – it's important to remember that anxiety levels are likely to peak for people in your life just before and just after making important decisions. Concerns – whether they are about profits, costs, customers or kids – will be at their highest point. To keep your relationship solid through these trying times, focus on helping ease those concerns. With Analyticals, the numbers and the details help.

ADAPTING YOUR STYLE FOR ANALYTICALS

One of the most important things to remember about adapting your Social Style is that at times the effort might make you a bit uncomfortable. After all, three out of four people in your life probably fit best in a Social Style different than yours.

Whatever your own style (which will be clearer to you after reading this book), you need to be thinking about how to adapt to ask-directed and task-directed behavior when dealing with Analyticals. Your

Checklist for Adapting Behaviors toward Analyticals

Try . . .	Avoid . . .
Preparing your case in advance.	Being disorganized or messy.
Sticking to business.	Spending much time on personal issues.
Supporting their principles. Use a thoughtful approach. Build your own credibility by listing the pros and cons for any suggestion you make.	Rushing the decision-making process.
Making an organized contribution to their efforts. Present specifics and do what you say you can do.	Being vague about what's expected of you or the other person, and not following through on what's expected of you.
Drawing up a scheduled approach to implementing a step-by-step action plan. Assure there will be no surprises.	Leaving things to chance or luck. Don't surprise Analyticals with new approaches to which they have not previously agreed.
Following through, if you agree.	Providing personal incentives.
Making an organized presentation of your position if you disagree about what will best serve the customer.	Using gimmicks or clever, quick manipulations.
Giving them time to verify the reliability of your actions. Be accurate and realistic.	Using unreliable sources. Being haphazard.
Providing solid, tangible, practical evidence.	Using someone else's opinion as testimony or evidence.
Providing time for thoroughness, when appropriate.	Pushing too hard or being unrealistic with deadlines.

goal is not to "become" an Analytical, if you are not one, but to adjust your style to theirs.

The central theme in increasing ask-directedness is quite logical: Ask more, tell less. No one enjoys being pushed into decisions, especially Analyticals.

Naturally, you will have to do some telling to establish your position and role in a relationship, but if you push too hard with Analyticals, resistance and relationship tension are likely to increase. Productivity will drop. Therefore, with Analyticals:

- *Ask for the opinions of others.* Make a point of asking plenty of guiding questions. Let the Analytical (and others who may also be part of the relationship) express their ideas. The most productive thing you can do with Analyticals is to ask questions aimed at understanding their needs and helping them get a clear picture of who you are and what you bring to the relationship. For example, it would be tell-directed to say, "This is what we are going to do." Instead, say, "I think the best thing to do would be. . . . What do you think?" Or, say, "I can think of three ways we can proceed, following path X, Y or Z. Do you see the same options, or are there others I have missed?"
- *Negotiate decision-making.* It's not enough to just let Analyticals have their say. They will tend to express their personal perspective couched in terms of objective data or technical issues. You need to listen for the feelings under the facts. It's vital to good communication with Analyticals that you acknowledge and value their unique point of view and expertise.
- *Listen without interrupting.* Patience is important, especially when dealing with people who are slow or reluctant to express their ideas, as Analyticals tend to be. Analyticals can also be concerned by details that others are not. Don't interrupt or dismiss these fine points, even if they seem irrelevant to the situation at the time. Analyticals need to be heard.

- *Adjust to the time needs of others.* A good sense of timing is as important as a sense of urgency. Be sensitive to the fact that some Analyticals may want a fair amount of time to evaluate an idea and think it through completely. Provide that opportunity.
- *Allow others to assume leadership roles.* Be careful with Analyticals not to infringe on their leadership roles or to question their knowledge and capabilities. Let them help create the agendas for your discussions, and provide sufficient opportunities for them to guide your conversations with their questions.

The main objective in adapting your behavior to accommodate the task-directedness of Analyticals is also quite logical: Focus first and foremost on what has to get done. Be careful about how much emotion you display and how much attention you pay to the people side of the issues you are dealing with. Take a serious, businesslike approach, without appearing cold or indifferent, using ideas, techniques, and approaches like these:

- *Talk less.* Fight any tendency you might have to monopolize conversation.
- *Restrain your enthusiasm.* If you show too much feeling you might come across as immature. Strive to display balance and self-control.
- *Make decisions based on fact.* It is important to operate based on what's going on in your head, not your "gut" when working with Analyticals. They prefer data to intuition. Learn to explain your recommendations by emphasizing facts and details.
- *Stop and think.* Don't be impulsive or hasty. Pause and reflect about important issues before speaking or acting. Make sure you're thinking logically.
- *Acknowledge the thoughts of others.* Focus your attention on the needs and expectations of Analyticals. If you are overly enthusiastic or expressive it can draw attention to you – and away from your mutual goals.

UNDERSTANDING AND HANDLING BACK-UP BEHAVIOR WITH ANALYTICALS

As described in Chapter 10, when tension in relationships reaches the point where people feel like saying, "I can't take it anymore," they begin exhibiting Back-Up Behavior. You are now at the moment when Versatility is needed most urgently. You are about to experience first-hand that moment of involuntary choice between "fight or flight."

Analyticals in Back-Up focus first on Avoiding Behaviors – flight. They manage excess tension by limiting their exposure to the stressful situation. The message you will get loud and clear is, "I don't want to talk about it now." It will be extremely difficult, if not impossible, to set up a meeting or to get a return phone call from an Analytical in Back-Up mode. If you do get a chance to meet or speak, this unhappy person will cut the session short, be reluctant to answer questions, and refuse to make a decision about – or even agree to consider – whatever has been the focus of your interactions.

You will find it helpful to return to Chapter 10 now to review the LSCPA model for dealing with Back-Up Behavior. As you do that, keep in mind that the goal in adapting LSCPA for Avoiding Behaviors is to *intervene*. Draw out people's feelings so that you can address issues in ways that will help release whatever tension has developed in your relationships.

Once you have used this process to head off a Back-Up situation, you can again begin to focus on the activities, problems, projects or whatever else defines the purpose of your relationship.

You will know you have helped restore comfort for Analyticals when they return to their characteristic behaviors. It may take some time and patience, but it's worth the investment.

Depending on how intense relationship tension becomes, the Back-Up Behavior of Analyticals, like all styles, can change. For example, watch for evidence that an unhappy Analytical who may have been avoiding you has begun Attacking behaviors. You can use the LSCPA model to modify your behaviors as needed to neutralize this reaction.

IF YOU ARE AN ANALYTICAL

If you are an Analytical, you may be reading this book with a bit of doubt. You may be interested in finding the evidence, intricacies, and proof about whether, how, and if this tool works. That thoroughness is a strength, but you'll want to take care not to take your doubt to extremes.

James Miller was immediately impressed when he was first exposed to Social Styles training. Still, he has Analytical leanings. He says he "didn't jump in emotionally with both feet at first."

James, a manager of software development for Qwest, first learned about Social Styles early in his career when working for Analyst International Corp. in Minneapolis in the US.

"Social Styles was an ingrained part of the culture of that company. I was the new kid on the block. I had the impression this was a good thing for the company, but it really wasn't an option for me to say, 'I don't believe in it.' I wasn't given the opportunity to be skeptical, although I tend to be that way.

"In short order, though, I saw that Social Styles had things you could take and use immediately. And it was based on a scientific process that's hard to dispute. I had been exposed to some personality assessment types of tools before learning Social Styles. At some level, the other tools struck me intellectually as being like horoscopes, overly broad and nothing I could really relate to. I was worried Social Styles might be the same sort of thing.

"But we used the concepts several times a week right away in making decisions about how to handle business situations, in strategizing and putting together sales proposals by thinking about the Social Styles of the people who were reading them, and I quickly understood the enthusiasm and positive spirit that were part of the organization's attitude about Social Styles."

If you are an Analytical, it is important to play to your strengths, continue to weigh the data and the alternatives in important relationships, and make practical decisions. But, as James learned, Versatility is important.

Strengths, Weaknesses and Misperceptions – Analyticals

Every Social Style has its strengths and weaknesses.

Strengths	Weaknesses
They create and find solid solutions because they rely on facts and logic.	They can be overly critical and picky.
They make thorough use of all available resources, which makes their solutions practical and persuasive.	They can belabor information gathering to the point of being indecisive.
They like to discover new ways to solve persistent problems.	They can be judgmental and moralistic.
They are competent at working out all details of a problem and then getting the job done right.	

Common Misperceptions about Analyticals

Two common misperceptions about Analyticals are that they don't have feelings and they don't know how to have fun. Analyticals are systematic thinkers, but we've been in enough emotional and high-energy situations with accountants, engineers and others who often fall into this style to tell you Analyticals are definitely not un-feeling, nor humorless.

If you are an Analytical and want to increase your Versatility:

- Take risks, or be willing to take shortcuts through procedures.
- Make decisions on the basis of intuition when appropriate.

SUMMARY

- Analyticals are ask-assertive and task-responsive. They approach the world asking questions and staying on task.

105

- Acting too tell-assertive or too personal with Analyticals can make you look unprofessional or cause discomfort.
- Save the small talk. Analyticals are not initially inclined to want to talk about things outside of the task at hand.
- Preparation and careful attention to detail are helpful in creating trust, comfort and confidence with Analyticals.
- Use guiding questions to influence Analyticals. And be specific.
- Listen for the feelings under the facts and encourage some discussion that taps into what Analyticals are thinking and feeling. It will help provide some balance and context to the factual information you will be trading.
- When adapting your behaviors to relate with Analyticals, remember that you are dealing with people who are ask- and task-directed in their assertiveness and responsiveness.
- Listen without interrupting when dealing with Analyticals. You may perceive them as being slow or reluctant to share information. They may need a little extra time, so be patient.
- Talk sparingly and strategically. Consciously avoid dominating the conversation.
- Analyticals in Back-Up tend initially toward flight. When they experience relationship tension, they want to avoid the source of the high levels of stress.
- If you are an Analytical and want to increase your Versatility, take a few risks and a few shortcuts. Develop your sense of intuition and let it influence some of your decision-making.

14 | Living and Working with Drivers

Being defeated is often a temporary condition. Giving up is what makes it permanent.

MARLENE VOS SAVANT

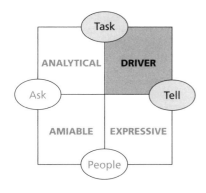

Driver. Even if you knew nothing about Social Styles, the word itself conjures strong images. Focus. Forcefulness. Certainty. Direction. Movement. Intensity.

Marilyn Smith is a long-time practitioner and teacher of Social Styles. As a senior facilitator and consultant in Wilson Learning's Extended Enterprise, she has been in countless business situations where she has taught or applied these concepts and tools and seen the payoff firsthand. She says the most dramatic impact she has experienced with Social Styles, however, is personal. With a Driver.

"My biggest success with Social Styles was in my relationship with my son, beginning when he was a teenager. He was a Driver, and I felt as if we were constantly at odds with one another. Our conversations were contentious and usually ended up with him coldly and loudly pushing back from our relationship, and me in tears, pleading emotionally for a little understanding.

"Using what I knew about Social Styles, I planned a different way to communicate with him – with no emotion. I decided I would simply state the facts and give him the bottom line on whatever we were discussing. I was amazed at his positive response.

"We got to the point we were able to work things out between us quickly and satisfactorily for both of us.

"At first, of course, I would then go to my room and cry because it had been so hard for me to handle things in a way that was designed to be comfortable for him, not me. But the turnaround in our relationship was so satisfying that I felt encouraged to continue. It became easier and helped us develop an excellent, close relationship. Now I know him for the person he really is inside – a big, soft teddy bear."

Drivers are tell-directed and task-directed on the assertiveness and responsiveness scales. This means they like the challenge of getting things done. They take charge, make quick decisions, and keep moving quickly toward results. It is entirely possible, as Marilyn discovered, that there can be a gentle person behind these kinds of hard-charging behaviors. As we've said before, Social Styles are based on observable behavior – what people do, not what they think or feel. But, like Analyticals, Drivers' behaviors are often first perceived as businesslike. They are even more results-oriented and far more likely to take initiative than Analyticals.

Drivers like to challenge new ideas and respond quickly to all situations. Just about everything they do will be straightforward, decisive and quick. As Marilyn figured out, Drivers prefer not to bring emotion into the communication equation. The teddy bear may be there on the inside, but it's most likely to hibernate until the situation is fully under control and headed in the right direction.

You'll notice that Drivers are people who seem most comfortable pursuing goals when they are in charge. These are the folks who have the knack for mapping out directions and having others see them to completion. Drivers are risk takers. They want to make things happen, and view every new problem as just another exciting challenge to handle. In fact, they thrive on challenge.

Drivers are described as people who:

- Are often direct and to the point with others.
- Seem to have strong opinions and convictions.
- Like to initiate, control and run on self-motivation.
- Tend to be efficient, hard working and focused on bottom-line results.

A Driver's strengths often include:

- Confidence, competence and a take-charge attitude.
- A willingness to take on new challenges and a preference for taking on things others often see as difficult to master.
- An ability to direct and productively coordinate the work of others.
- A sense of responsibility for making things happen.

Drivers are independent, action-oriented and want to be in control. That is a powerful and quick combination that can sometimes lead to the misperception that Drivers are impersonal, pushy and hard-hearted. They do have feelings; they just don't always show them.

DRIVER EXPECTATIONS

"Don't take it personally. It's only business."

If you are ever likely to hear those words from the lips of someone you know, they most likely will be spoken by a person whose behaviors are best captured in the Driver quadrant of the Social Styles matrix. Even the short, punchy sentences say "Driver."

The time you have to make a first impression with a Driver will be extremely brief, and the reaction at the end of that time will be swift and decisive. Your prospects of establishing or enhancing relationships with Drivers are likely to fade quickly if you initially come across as making frivolous use of their time. Forget amiability. Stay away from any behaviors that might make you appear overly smooth, slick or

The Driver Social Style

Businesslike. Results-oriented. Likely to take charge and take initiative. Likes challenges. Makes quick decisions. Direct and to the point. Strong opinions and convictions. Hard-working. Efficient. Confident and competent. Productively co-ordinates the work of others. Likely to challenge new ideas. Quick to respond. Inclined to correct, modify or add to others' ideas. Straightforward. Responsible. Makes things happen.

Verbal and Nonverbal Cues	Serious. Formal posture. Restrained gestures. Rapid speech. Direct. Voice inflection varies little, usually only to emphasize important points.
Work Style	Independent.
Attitude about Time	"Use it efficiently to get desired results."
Attitude about Accomplishment	"Achieve strong results in the shortest time possible."
Attitude about Others	"Relationships are important but secondary until a task is defined and competency to deal with it is established."
Natural Work Activity Strengths	Initiating and monitoring.
Personal Motivator	Power: Seeks to control the tangible resources of a project such as time, budget, people. Prefers to be given options and probabilities and allowed to make own decisions. Values receiving more authority, control or power over the situation or environment.
Common Misperceptions about Drivers	Impersonal and pushy because they focus on tasks and control their emotions.

glib. No matter how careful you believe you are in nurturing personal connections, Drivers are perhaps the most difficult people to connect with on that level, at least in the initial stages of a relationship.

As Marilyn learned with her son, it helps to get on quickly with the business of demonstrating that you understand and can address "the big picture" of what you are dealing with in your relationships with Drivers. Make it clear with them that you will act in ways that will have a positive influence on their bottom line – the things that are most important to them. Do whatever you need to do by the time you say it will be done. And stick to providing only the most relevant information.

Drivers, like Analyticals, are task-directed, but unlike Analyticals, are not interested in understanding every nuance and every piece of data related to the work or issues around which your relationship is built.

Don't misinterpret that characteristic of Drivers, however, to mean you don't have to worry about the details. In the end, you will have to be thorough, on target, and in control of every aspect of the elements and activities important to your relationship. If not, Drivers, who typically are not prone to reveal much about their thoughts or feelings through expressions or gestures, might become very demonstrative in showing you the way out of their lives.

Drivers can be charming, but most often people in this tell-directed, task-directed quadrant of the Social Styles matrix don't focus on presenting an air of friendliness, nor do they expect it from the people with whom they deal.

So, be prepared, be well informed about Drivers' circumstances, and be ready to be challenged.

Drivers expect you to:

- *Be task-oriented.* With Drivers, business comes before relationships.
- *Make the most efficient use of their time.* Drivers tend to be busy people with tight agendas. If you get time in that schedule, use it efficiently.

- *Provide insightful information early in your personal encounters.* Drivers are very interested in facts and well-documented reasons why and how you might fit into their lives and business. These are people who are more rational than emotional. They want to learn about benefits, and they expect the information you provide will be germane and accurate so they can quickly evaluate the value of a potential relationship with you.

- *Tailor your ideas to address their concerns and issues.* Drivers have a strong grasp of what they need and want, and they expect your ideas to support their agendas. If your plan veers too far from what they have in mind, you must be prepared to show how you and your ideas ultimately advance their purpose. It's not that they want to be unique. They want to enhance their sense of power or need for control.

- *Offer choices and options in a way that allows them to feel they are making the ultimate decision.* Drivers desire control and may balk if they feel you are questioning or threatening their power or authority in any way. Even if you come up with all the best ideas in your relationships with Drivers, you are more likely to earn their trust and fondness if you can sacrifice a few strokes to your own ego in order to make it clear they are in charge.

- *Provide them with the odds for success when you ask them to take risks.* Drivers thrive on control, so they do not want to be blindsided by something unexpected. They don't want to be overburdened with too many details about a project. But fair warning about how likely it is something could go wrong – and where such a failure might lead – would be the kind of relevant information Drivers want.

ENTRY WITH DRIVERS

Trust, comfort and confidence are essential to strong relationships, as we said when we introduced our Entry/Dialogue/Closure concepts. Keeping in mind it takes time to build this kind of credibility and connection with people, it is vital to begin working on it early – in the Entry stage.

In the Entry stage with Drivers:

- Establish a quick pace from the moment you meet Drivers. Don't, however, neglect to give sufficient time to build trust with them. This can be a challenging balancing act.
- Listen and focus your complete attention on the Driver's ideas, interests, and objectives.
- Present only factual evidence that relates to the Drivers' situations and what you bring to the relationships. Focus directly on the benefits to them.
- Arrive on time, or even a bit early. Begin on time. Stay on task. Finish on time, or better yet, end early to earn extra appreciation. Punctuality will pay off for you with Drivers.
- Get down to business immediately. Avoid small talk.
- Be prepared to provide plenty of information, but give it out carefully. Present the most relevant material, then dole out additional ideas and data only at the request of the Driver. Drivers want to get to the bottom line quickly, but at times will want to know the factual basis for your ideas, plans, and conclusions relevant to your relationship. Although early encounters with Drivers may focus on "the big picture," be ready to provide on demand the kind of detail you would normally prepare for communicating with an Analytical.
- Be personable, but keep your gestures and facial expressions to a minimum. Speak firmly, but strive to maintain a level tone in your voice. Some Drivers appear almost deadpan and expressionless in business situations and they expect more or less the same thing from everyone else. Create an environment of reserve and relative formality.
- Structure your Purpose, Process and Payoff thoughts and statements (described in Chapter 11) about your meetings to suit tell-directed,

task-directed behavior preferences. Make your introduction at each contact businesslike and to the point. Include some of the key facts and figures related to the projects, activities or other concerns central to the relationship. Demonstrate your intent to be quick, thorough and complete. Emphasize the bottom line as it pertains to the issue at hand.

Establishing your credibility (as described in Chapter 11) with Drivers will also be different from what you do with the other styles:

- As with all styles, you will need to establish your credibility with Drivers. However, with Drivers you will often need to do it more quickly.
- *Propriety:* As with Analyticals, drivers will expect more formal work behavior and appearance. Dressing and behaving slightly more conservatively than the situation calls for might be the best approach for a first meeting.
- *Competence:* Drivers are mostly likely to judge your competence through your results. Stories about recent successes are valuable here, but with a focus less on what you accomplished and more on the outcomes achieved. Drivers are likely to want to hear about specific factual results and impact.
- *Commonality.* Focus on commonalities related to a task, and specifically, on commonality on the value of the outcome over the process. While an Amiable or Expressive might like to hear about your latest golf game, a Driver who plays golf will be more interested in your score and handicap, so forgo the story about how you lost your ball in the rough.
- *Intent.* Express your positive intent for the relationship in a factual way with emphasis on what you will do to meet that intent. Drivers want to know that your company takes responsibility for customer satisfaction, but more to the point, they want to know that you achieve it, and what action you will take to assure it.

DIALOGUE WITH DRIVERS

Your intent in the very important Dialogue stage is to figure out what matters to the other person, and to find mutual solutions and opportunities for building your relationships. It's also the point when you gauge your own sense of how well what you know, can do, or have to offer matches those needs and interests.

In the Dialogue stage with Drivers:

- Ask questions that allow the Driver to direct the interaction. Questions such as "How would you like to approach this problem?" or "What do you believe the ultimate goal should be for this team?" will allow Drivers to get out important information quickly.
- Ask fact-finding questions that will help you understand what they value and reward.
- Clarify priorities.
- Make your line of questioning consistent with the objective of your interaction, whether it's a phone call or a face-to-face meeting.
- Keep a fast pace and stay on time.
- Follow up immediately on any requests for additional information.
- Support their beliefs and decisions. Make clear how you can have a positive influence in areas of importance to them.
- Clarify their expectations about next steps.

Remember to refer back to Chapter 11 for specific recommendations on questioning and listening skills for Drivers in the Dialogue stage.

CLOSURE WITH DRIVERS

One of the great challenges with Drivers is to maintain their interest and loyalty. Of all Social Styles types, Drivers are likely to be the fastest to seek a replacement or an alternative to what you bring to a relationship – if you don't make a quick, positive impression. They know there are many people who do what you do or have the skills and talents you have, and they will make swift decisions about moving on if you don't prove you have done your homework in knowing what they want and need – the work done in the Dialogue stage. Drivers tend to dislike reversing decisions, so do your best to continually meet expectations when you are in the Closure stage.

Up until this point in your efforts to create or enhance a relationship, you are working to uncover the needs, desires, and preferences of the other person. The Closure stage is when you find ways to move the other person to the point of believing strongly in who you are and what you do and coming to agreement about what you will do together.

Affirming

- Provide documented options that demonstrate the value of your ideas and plans.
- Focus on the quality of your ideas, the depth of your experience, and the value of what you bring to the relationship.
- Be specific and factual, but don't overwhelm with details.
- Appeal to their need to take independent action. Drivers prefer to be forthright in their decision-making, so reinforce their perceptions of their strengths and capabilities.
- Summarize quickly. Allow them to choose a course of action. Highlight the options, and leave the final decision up to them.
- Be direct. Express your needs for actions and commitments in clear, factual terms.

Supporting

At times during Closure, you will need to reassure co-workers, colleagues, and customers you will be there to hold up the relationship in good times or bad. Drivers generally need a sense of that support that is quicker and crisper than most, because they are inclined to swift action if they are uncomfortable in a relationship. To reaffirm your relationship and let Drivers know you will be there for them and be able to provide what they need from you:

- Act immediately on any commitments you make.
- Keep to the schedule and other important agreements – there should be no surprises.
- Make all your communication quick and to the point.
- Set and communicate checkpoints and milestones.
- Be prepared to make changes and concessions in any agreements you reach with Drivers. They sometimes attach conditions to their negotiations.
- Offer time to consider next steps, options, or action plans.
- Anticipate objections in advance. You're quite likely to hear some. Come prepared with facts, figures, examples, case histories and reference materials that can help address any doubts or reservations about whatever you are addressing.
- Don't call, write or drop in to check on Drivers unless there is a real need to do so.

Enhancing

It might seem as if coming into a relationship providing a ready-made decision would meet a Driver's need for speed, but be careful not to take decision-making options and powers away from them. Close every loophole. Make sure there are no clouds hanging over the project or the data. Offer your ideas – without any wildly speculative guarantees or promises. Then, step back to provide the space and time Drivers need to take control and make their decisions.

Whether you are negotiating project plans, developing an important meeting agenda, or making a sale with a Driver, if you feel you have won your point, fight the urge to slip into small talk as you wrap up your discussions in this stage. No matter how good you feel about the work you've done in earning the rewards of this relationship, it definitely isn't time to relax and act as if you have reached some new level of personal intimacy. Gather up your materials, pack your briefcase, shut down your computer and head off to take care of the next steps without slowing down to socialize. That's what Drivers would do.

- Check to make sure Drivers believe they are getting what you promise. Are they satisfied with the value of what you are bringing to the relationship?
- Ensure you deliver whatever results you promise.
- Make things easier for Drivers. Avoid getting them overly involved in the aspects of your relationship for which you are primarily responsible.

Perhaps the most important things to remember in helping Drivers be comfortable and confident in their relationships with you are to be quick, clear, and on target.

ADAPTING YOUR STYLE FOR DRIVERS

Demonstrating your Versatility with Drivers – your ability to adapt your behaviors to make them feel comfortable – requires behaviors on your part that accommodate their preference to be tell-directed on the assertiveness scale and task-directed on the responsiveness scale.

What's the main strategy for moving your own behavior more to the tell-directed side of the assertiveness scale? Fewer questions, more answers. Tell more often. Ask less often.

The main strategy for being more task-directed on the responsiveness scale will sound similar: Focus on what must get done, with as little emotion as possible. Allow the Driver to take the lead on moving toward more personal topics. Task-directed people (the Drivers and Analyticals) do talk about personal things, but usually after they feel that the task has been dealt with. Let Drivers decide when the task issues have been completed.

People who are Amiable or Expressive try to influence with expression and feelings. Drivers often perceive this as the behavior of someone who is too emotionally involved in a situation. To influence Drivers, you must use a businesslike approach. You must be serious, but not appear cold or indifferent. To further increase the comfort of Drivers:

Checklist for Adapting Behaviors toward Drivers

Try . . .	Avoid . . .
Being clear, specific, brief and to the point.	Rambling on or wasting time.
Approaching them in a straightforward, direct way – sticking to business in a pleasant but professional manner.	Being demonstrably excited, casual, informal or unprofessional.
Coming prepared with objectives and support materials in a well-organized package.	Forgetting or losing things, and doing things that confuse or distract.
Presenting the facts clearly and logically and planning your presentation for efficiency.	Leaving gaps or cloudy, uncertain issues.
Asking specific "what" questions.	Asking rhetorical or irrelevant questions or repeating them accidentally.
Providing alternatives that allow them to make their own final decisions.	Arriving with a ready-made decision that you've made.
Providing facts and figures related to the probability of success and the potential effectiveness of each of the options you propose.	Wildly speculating or offering guarantees and assurances that you risk not being able to fulfill.
Taking issues with the facts, not the person, if you disagree on something. Supporting the results, not the person, if you agree.	Letting a disagreement be reflected on a personal level.
Motivating and persuading by referring to objectives and results that your customer has identified previously.	Trying to convince by personal means or emotional appeals.
Departing graciously after finishing your business.	Telling stories and getting chummy after finishing business.

- *Talk less.* Don't monopolize the conversation. Learn to listen more.
- *Restrain your enthusiasm.* Drivers sometimes see excessive displays of emotion as a sign of immaturity. Strive for balance and control.
- *Make decisions based on facts.* It doesn't pay with Drivers – or Analyticals, as you learned earlier – to operate on "gut feeling" or instinct rather than logic. Use your head. Explain your recommendations using facts for emphasis.
- *Stop and think.* You need to be quick, but not impulsive or hasty. Pause and reflect on important issues before acting or speaking. That will help keep your emotions in check.
- *Acknowledge the thoughts of others.* Zero in on the needs and expectations of Drivers. Recognize their good ideas in ways that show the relationship is not all about you.

UNDERSTANDING AND HANDLING BACK-UP BEHAVIOR WITH DRIVERS

When you are off track with Drivers, it doesn't take very long for them to reach that dangerous, tense point in the relationship where they are saying out loud or through their behaviors, "I can't take it anymore."

When it comes to relieving relationship tension, most Drivers first opt for the *fight* rather than the *flight* option. They become Autocratic, confronting, demanding, focusing even more intensely than normal on the issue, and looking harder than ever for a rational explanation for the situation.

Drivers manage extreme tension in relationships by trying to assert even more control than normal. Their basic message to you will be, "I am not going to do it this way. If you can't do it my way, this relationship is finished." Their tone may be righteous, imposing, and cold, and they will use their rank and intensified reason to make sure you get the message that they have no interest in letting you move the relationship forward. Their unwillingness to let the relationship develop further will be displayed for you in a way that has a definite ring of finality.

The Listen-Share-Clarify-Problem Solve-Ask for Action (LSCPA) model described in Chapter 10 is the place to turn at this point, but be assured you face a significant challenge in working to undo a decision a Driver makes under this kind of stress. The key to saving relationships with unhappy Drivers is to concentrate your efforts on *neutralizing* their battle-focused behaviors.

Neutralize Drivers' tensions by letting them vent. Usually the comments you will hear sound like a lot of task-directed demands ("Here's what you'll do to make this right. Call your team together now, no matter what else they are doing, and get them to finish this project as promised before the end of the day."). Let them express their needs and expectations, and then use LSCPA to focus on how to accomplish what they want. They'll tell you the *what* emphatically. You need to get to the *how*. But you can't get to the *how* until you've let them voice their anger and frustration.

As you use these tools with Drivers, remember they want control. They are forceful, results-oriented people. Whatever you do to recover and try to restore comfort for a distressed Driver, efficiency and effectiveness will always be important, as will a sense of urgency and a willingness to deal unemotionally with even the toughest issues.

IF YOU ARE A DRIVER

If you are a Driver, you may already be eager to be done reading *The Social Styles Handbook* so you can get about the business of putting what you have learned into practice. You may have flipped forward through the next chapters to see what still lies ahead. You may have even taken to skim reading, looking for the high points, gleaning what you can from the charts, graphics, and headlines, making some quick and incisive deductions about what this all means for you. You get it, and now you want to get on with it.

These are some of your strengths. You are focused, quick, decisive, and action-oriented. And you should continue to emphasize these behaviors.

Strengths, Weaknesses and Misperceptions – Drivers

Every Social Style has its strengths and weaknesses.

Strengths	Weaknesses
They provide clear expectations.	They can be pushy.
They offer solutions based on facts and options.	They can be unwilling to take time to listen.
They produce results efficiently and effectively.	They sometimes don't value the positions and view points of others.
They are focused, decisive, timely and concise.	They can emphasize control to the point of creating tension, compliance or apprehension in others.
They act quickly.	
They are responsive to challenges.	

Common Misperceptions about Drivers

A common misperception about Drivers is that they are impersonal, pushy, and callous because they focus so intensely on tasks and tend to control their emotions. The intention of most Drivers is to take care of business as quickly and efficiently as possible, not necessarily to be bossy about getting it done. And, whether the emotions show or not, Drivers have them. They just try not to let feelings influence their actions excessively.

James Miller, a Driver, says he has learned, however, that in his role as a supervisor of software development for Qwest he has to fight the urge to bulldoze ahead on his own just because he's certain he knows what has to be done. "I can't be the one who always follows through on situations when I think I know the right answer, even when that seems to be the easiest and quickest way to get something accomplished. I can't just step into a situation with the people I lead and say, 'Here is the way it should be done.'

"There are times when I believe I know the solution to a particular challenge, but still spend a lot of time talking to people to see if we come around to the same conclusion. It's far more effective for our relationships and our team success in the long run if we sit down and go through a process of mutual discovery and evaluation."

Part of that process of mutual discovery, James says, is valuing the diversity that people of different Social Styles bring to the team. Acknowledging the importance of those differences means that he often has to talk to different people in different ways to achieve the same objective.

"We may be in a situation when I need the whole team to work a lot of overtime. If I'm talking about that with an Amiable person, who's ask-directed and people-directed, I may emphasize that this is something we need to do collectively as part of a team effort, that we will all be giving up other things for the common good, that there is an end in sight, and that we soon will be getting back to the other things that are important and that we believe in – such as balance in our lives. With an Analytical person, who's ask-directed and task-directed, I might start out by dealing more with the facts of the situation – lay out the deadlines for the tasks that remain to be done and talk about the progress we've already made."

If you are a Driver, several other important things you can do to increase your Versatility and improve your ability to build relationships with people of other Social Styles are:

- Show patience when others try to express the merits of their ideas.
- Engage in thorough analysis of situations.
- Ask for others' ideas and opinions.
- Listen more.
- Share and respond to personal feelings.
- Allow others to take the lead at times.

123

SUMMARY

- Drivers are tell- and task-directed. They are businesslike, results oriented, like to initiate things and control situations, appear confident but don't show a lot of emotion, and value power and options.

- They expect you to be serious, well prepared, efficient, and they form their first impressions quickly. They need "the big picture" and prize rational benefits. Offer them options so they can feel their decision- making will lead to success.

- In Entry, the trust-building stage, keep a quick pace and get to the point, and focus on benefits and outcomes. Remain formal. Know your facts but don't dwell on details.

- In the Dialogue stage, when you are defining problems and needs, use questions to give the Driver the lead, then clarify and prioritize, and keep the pace brisk. Show how you can help Drivers reach their goals.

- In the Closure stage, when you are moving Drivers to agreements, present options, give room for independent action, and document the benefits of what you have to offer over the alternative solutions or resources. Anticipate objections.

- During Closure, reaffirm your support for the relationship quickly, and follow up on all your commitments. Keep things on schedule, work to ensure satisfaction and handle the logistics in a way that will allow Drivers to stay minimally involved with the details.

- Drivers in Back-Up first adopt Autocratic behavior, the fight response. Neutralize their tension by letting them vent, listening for how you can set things right.

- If you are a Driver, patience and thorough analysis of tricky situations will increase the perception of your Versatility, as will your efforts to involve others in leading and decision-making.

15 | Living and Working with Amiables

If you want one year of prosperity, grow grain. If you want 10 years of prosperity, grow trees. If you want 100 years of prosperity, grow people.

CHINESE PROVERB

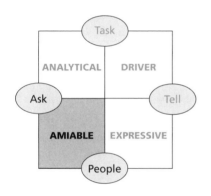

In some ways, relationships with Amiables, the people in the ask-directed, people-directed quadrant of the Social Style matrix, can be among the most complex to understand and manage.

That may seem counter-intuitive. The first thoughts that come to mind when you think of amiability center on harmony, compatibility, and striving to make sure everybody's needs are well met and everybody is happy. But that's why relationships with these people can get complicated. Amiables want so much to keep their relationships with you running smoothly, they'll not always show it when things are actually running into trouble. When Amiables encounter pressure or conflict, you many not get many warning signs from them, and therefore your relationship may stall without your really knowing it's happening. It may seem as if things are going along well between you, except that there seems to be an unexplained, persistent and unproductive lag in action steps and decision-making. And when you do notice the relationship is faltering, your

Amiable acquaintance may not be letting you know why. Indeed, an Amiable may appear quite comfortable in a relationship with you, all the while being troubled by other aspects of the relationship, especially those pertaining to its connections to others. It's not unusual in a sales situation, for example, for an Amiable customer to give a salesperson clear indications a purchase agreement is imminent, but then continually delay the decision out of concern for what others in his or her company might think about the deal.

So here is what you need to know about Amiables.

Like Analyticals, Amiables are ask-directed, but the questions they bring to their work are often more focused, at least initially, on the people involved in a task than the task itself. Amiables are concerned with cooperating, providing support and reaching agreement. An important step in pursuing a relationship with Amiables often is to establish strong personal ties with the Amiables, but also with others involved in the work or issues that will be central to your interactions.

Amiables are often perceived as the quiet, unassuming members in a team or group. They provide a sort of social lubricant in their circles of influence. They are warm, friendly listeners, who are easy to get along with, and who enjoy personal contact and shared responsibility.

The traits that describe Amiables include these:

- They accept others easily and place a high priority on getting along.
- They like to minimize interpersonal conflict whenever possible.
- They are easy to get to know and easy to work with.
- They appear quiet, cooperative and supportive.

The strengths Amiables bring to the workplace include:

- Giving good advice and counsel.
- Helping where needed, and providing positive comments about the work, contributions and accomplishment of others.

The Amiable Style

Quiet. Unassuming. Supportive. Warm. Friendly listeners. Easy to get along with. Enjoys personal contact. Shares responsibility. Concerned about collaboration, providing support, and reaching agreement. Requires extensive data for decision-making. Prefers to have consensus before moving ahead. Often focuses on personal ties before goals.

Verbal and Nonverbal Cues	Warm, friendly and open. Relaxed posture. Slow speech. Pleasant and soft voice. Open and eager facial expressions.
Work Style	With others.
Attitude about Time	"Take time to establish relationships and to make steady progress through a slow, sure pace."
Attitude about Accomplishment	"Results come through people working together."
Attitude about Others	"People are the most important asset in any project and collaborating with others is the best way to get things done."
Natural Work Activity Strengths	Coaching and counseling.
Personal Motivator	Approval: Seeks to promote or gain agreement from others and to be included as part of the group or team. Values receiving others' approval and having a positive impact on others.
Common Misperceptions about Amiables	Places too much emphasis on relationships, move too slowly, and doesn't get results.

- Communicating high levels of trust and confidence in others.
- Making people feel comfortable about themselves.

Amiables are not inclined to move ahead without strong support from others to back them up, so they are sometimes misperceived as risk averse and slow decision makers. They want time to build relationships, and they prefer plenty of feedback and cooperation before saying yes or no to anything important.

Connecting closely with Amiables is something of an art. Their openness and interest in personal relationships makes them behave very collegially towards just about everyone, yet, as we said at the beginning of this chapter, at times that sensitivity to others can lead them to disguise signs of trouble. Amiables present unique challenges.

AMIABLE EXPECTATIONS

You will probably never meet people more willing to listen to you than Amiables, but you must take care with what you say, and how and when you say it. Amiables, even those with strong needs for what you can bring to a relationship, will want to get to know you personally before talking business, making commitments, or getting involved in any kind of project or issue with you. More than people of other styles, Amiables prefer to know people on a personal level before they get "serious." You will need to sell yourself to Amiables a bit before you can persuade them toward anything else that might be on your agenda for the relationship.

In work situations, Amiables will listen receptively, so plan to proceed slowly, and be certain to use some of that time to share information about you that goes beyond what would normally be considered "professional." Building relationships with Amiables is not about making friends, but it may feel that way at times. Don't lose sight of your ultimate personal or professional goals in communicating with Amiables, but be prepared to open up and connect on a far more personal level than with people of most other Social Styles. For Amiables, this is an important step in them coming to the point where they know you well enough to trust what you say.

For example, if you walk into the office of a new co-worker who is an Amiable, it can be very helpful to your relationship to take note of the personal effects on the desk or the walls. If you see a photo that shows your new colleague's son or daughter in a graduation cap and gown, this is a good time to ask about the occasion. If there is a book about golf on the shelf next to the company handbook, and you are a golfer, your new co-worker will probably be very interested to know your handicap or your favorite place to play. With a Driver you might just make a mental note about what those kinds of clues indicate about a person, but with Amiables you can bring them into the conversation. That will give them a chance to share more about themselves, but it will also allow you to casually provide insights about yourself.

Amiables expect you to:

- *Be open and honest.* Amiables function well in situations where there are no hidden agendas, but they will be uncomfortable if you take a cold, get-right-down-to-business approach with them.
- *Spend time developing a relationship.* Amiables function best when there is little or no relationship tension by the time you begin to tackle the task at hand. They want to see progress toward goals, but are far more comfortable than Drivers and Expressives with moving ahead at a steady, deliberate pace.
- *Be congenial and prove you are trustworthy.* Establish your reputation with Amiables early in your relationship; it's something they value. Don't rush your relationship or create too much pressure about your agenda. That will cause Amiables to shy away from you.
- *Provide reassurance about who you are and what you believe.* Amiables are very interested in working and developing relationships with people who share their values and challenges.
- *Give personal support.* Amiables look for signs of willingness to accept personal responsibility and to provide personal support. In

collaborating with you, they are not only doing business or completing a project. They are building a relationship. Amiables want personal assurances from you as an individual. React and respond to their personal feelings and offer support and attention for the issues that matter to them most.

- *Provide guarantees and assurances.* Amiables are not risk-takers. They work deliberately and sometimes cautiously. Help them eliminate any worries they may have about the appropriateness of their decisions and the correctness of their actions.

ENTRY WITH AMIABLES

Building trust with people is always an important first step in communicating and building relationships, but it is especially critical with Amiables, and it will take more than being able to establish your credentials. Relax. Be natural. Be patient. With Amiables, it will seem like they are not very concerned about time and deadlines. But it is important to view time and deadlines from the Amiable's point of view. To an Amiable, you are saving time in the future by establishing trust early on in the relationship. For Amiables, the pressure as deadlines approach is easier to deal with when they can trust, on a personal level, the people they work with. They prefer to work with people with whom they have established a relationship that allows open discussion of issues.

So, open up and use this warming-up period to let them know who you are – inside and outside of your "official" role.

In the Entry stage with Amiables:

- Make "small talk." Engage in informal conversation before getting down to business.
- Ask questions about their work and personal goals. Listen actively to demonstrate a personal interest. Use plenty of facial expressions and body language that show your reactions to what you are hearing. Give verbal reactions. Ask clarifying questions that show you

are paying close attention, and tie in some of your own experiences that relate to what you are hearing.

- If you have common acquaintances, mention them, especially if you have a relationship similar to the one you are trying to develop.
- Establish a slow, comfortable pace in your meetings. People are the first priority with Amiables; tasks come next.
- Don't try to establish yourself or what you bring to the relationship, project or issue you may be addressing as being revolutionary or cutting edge. Amiables want to deal with things that are special, but even more importantly, they want to deal with people with a solid foundation and reputation. They want to know they can count on you. They want to be certain you will be there to support them if there are any problems.

Don't rush into your Purpose, Process and Payoff statements (de-scribed in Chapter 11) with Amiables. Take some time to warm up the conversation with some personal talk. Remember that Amiables are ask-directed and people-directed. As you talk about why you are to-gether and what you want to accomplish, encourage questions. Also, take into account the impact your ideas or actions may have on other people about whom the Amiable may be concerned, and provide as-surances you are aware of their needs and interests.

DIALOGUE WITH AMIABLES

Amiables know you need information from them in order for you to collaborate effectively. In fact, if you make the right initial impres-sion, Amiables often will be very willing to share what you need. But willingness and good intentions still don't mean the same thing as fast. You may be eager to understand an Amiable's circumstances or point of view on an issue for all the right reasons – you want to help solve their problems, improve bottom-line results, or improve the quality of his or her life – but you must still tend to the personal as-pect of the relationship. It's better to assume that you are still in the

Entry phase when you are doing the Dialogue step, especially with Amiables.

Dialogue, as you have learned earlier, is a critical stage in getting to know someone – the period when you are learning about what matters most to the other person. With Amiables, however, this exploration must include enough time for them to feel comfortable about the process of uncovering the personal factors that will influence the relationship, whether it is personal or professional.

Amiables are ask-directed, so you will have to dig for your information. First, though, you have to set the right personal tone.

In the Dialogue stage with Amiables:

- Use pacing, tone of voice, and body language to create a relaxed and cooperative atmosphere. Share information and feelings, and ask questions to get at the same for Amiables. You want to create an open, warm exchange.
- Listen responsively. Give plenty of verbal and nonverbal feedback, especially when you hear information helpful in understanding the business challenges and issues you want to help resolve.
- Ask questions specifically related to achieving long-term goals that are mutual to your relationship. Amiables, who often are averse to risk and predominantly attuned to the present moment, tend to understate these kinds of far-reaching objectives.
- Determine if there are financial issues that will influence your relationship. Because Amiables are people-directed and ask-directed, financial issues sometimes don't automatically surface on their lists of concerns. If you believe these kinds of issues can make or break your relationship you will have to ask about them to make sure they are aired.
- Find out who else might be affected by decisions made or actions taken as a result of your relationship with an Amiable. Amiables will frequently seek out quite a bit of support from key people in

their lives before making decisions. If you know others will be involved in helping an Amiable make final decisions, you must also involve them in the Dialogue process. Their needs and interests must be reflected in your intentions and actions.

- Summarize and feed back what you believe to be an Amiable's key ideas and feelings. Confirm you have understood and touched on the things most important to his or her situation.

Don't be surprised if an Amiable suggests you talk to others as well, and don't make the mistake of not following through. Amiables will want all opinions and ideas heard. Sometimes, when people of other styles suggest you do discovery with other stakeholders in a situation, it can be an effort to "pass you off" to someone else. This is rarely true with Amiables. So if an Amiable suggests you meet with others or requests a group discussion, treat this as a positive opportunity to meet the Amiable's need for shared responsibility and collaboration.

Establishing your credibility (as described in Chapter 11) with Amaibles will also be different from what you do with the other styles:

- Establishing your credibility (as described in Chapter 11) with Amiables requires not only being able to demonstrate your ability to do the work, but also careful attention to the people-directed side of the equation
- *Propriety:* With Amiables it is not just about meeting their expectations around customs and appearance, but also what the Amiable thinks *others* expect. In choosing your approach and appearance, pay attention to the work environment, and try to match it as closely as possible.
- *Competence:* Testimonials from others who can speak to your competence goes much further with an Amiable that does a list of degrees

and experiences. Better yet if those testimonials can come from people he or she knows, or knows of.

- *Commonality.* Commonality is important to Amiables, so it is important to establish this early. Focus on commonalities as it relates to values and character, particular the value of collaboration and involvement of others. An Amiable will be more interested in knowing that you share, for example, the value of family, than that you share an interest in rock climbing.
- *Intent.* With all styles it is important to express your positive intent. Particularly for an Amiable, positive personal intent matters a lot. An Amiable wants to know that your company takes responsibility for customer satisfaction, but is more concerned that you personally will take responsibility for that satisfaction. The phrase "I don't care how much you know until I know how much you care" was likely first spoken by an Amiable.

CLOSURE WITH AMIABLES

Amiables make specific decisions, agreements, and commitments differently than people of other Social Styles.

It's part of their strength that they are deliberate and effective at involving others in their projects. They coach. They counsel. They are supportive and helpful to others.

Amiables are loyal and dedicated to the people they work with, and are generous with doling out compliments and credit for the accomplishments and contributions of others. In turn, they look to colleagues to provide the same kind of help, support, and approval for their efforts.

For you, that means building your relationship may be a bit more complicated. Don't oversimplify your reaction to what is happening. It is not that Amiables can't make decisions, or won't make decisions; rather, it's that they make decisions only when they are confident that they are satisfying everybody who will be affected by their decisions.

Affirming

- Show how you, your ideas, and your actions will affect all the people involved with the tasks or objectives that are the focus of your relationship.
- Provide a clear rationale for why you and what you bring to the relationship are resources and assets that will serve the Amiable's interest – in the present and the future.
- Use references and examples of your competence to establish your credibility. Amiables take comfort in knowing you have experiences that might be to their benefit.
- When making agreements with Amiables, give guarantees. Provide contingency plans that will take into account as many likely scenarios as you can. Show Amiables how you can cover all the possible situations that might develop and what you can do to provide whatever protection could be needed.
- Ask for commitments indirectly. Go easy.
- When collaborating on a project or task, clearly define – in writing – who will do what and by when to move the process to a final decision and then to implementation. Spell out the details of your personal involvement in the overall project, the commitment of resources required of you and the Amiable, as well as the expectations for the Amiable's involvement in the completion of the process and project.
- Get a commitment, even if you have to get it based on a contingency. This will help keep Amiables from drifting away from making a final decision.

Supporting

It's quite clear, especially if you are an Expressive or a Driver, that communicating and building relationships with Amiables requires a large dose of patience. It's equally important, however, to mix in a good-sized helping of persistence. Amiables often need help to keep the decision-making process moving. You won't be able to skip any steps or bypass any key people when you are working with Amiable, but the faster you can provide the information and comfort they require – for themselves and their fellow stakeholders – the faster you can help them make a commitment in their own minds.

- Don't pressure them to make decisions.
- Don't corner them.
- Don't force them to respond too quickly. Avoid saying things such as, "Here's how I see it."
- Don't position yourself or your ideas as new or unique. Amiables typically don't want to be "the first" at anything. That indicates risk.
- Help them earn support for their decisions from other stakeholders. Amiables function best when they have support from key people in their lives.
- Handle the details. Be mindful that Amiables are not big risk-takers. They will want to be comfortable knowing every necessary step related to what you are addressing in your relationship has been carefully considered. Taking care of those kinds of details themselves is not a strength or a preference for Amiables.
- Assure that whatever you agree to accomplish together goes smoothly and problem free. Provide periodic progress reports to show Amiables things are going well enough to keep everybody happy.
- Arrange for back-up support, extra resources or whatever else is needed to maintain their comfort, especially in the early stages of whatever actions you plan to take together.
- Support the Amiable's need to involve all those other people in the process of making a final decision. Allow yourself plenty of time for this phase of negotiations.
- Work out any problems agreeably. Listen carefully to any concerns Amiables have, even if they seem trivial.

Enhancing

Everything you've learned so far about Amiables should be a good reminder that the Entry/Dialogue/Closure model is not strictly a linear process. Enhancing your relationship is generally an important step in the Closure phase, but this kind of investment and reaffirmation can begin long before you ever feel as if you have earned a commitment to a relationship from someone. Indeed, with Amiables, it is important to show your support and value for the relationship early and make it an ongoing priority.

- Make Amiables feel good about themselves for the decisions they have made with you. Congratulate them. Be aware that Amiables are very susceptible to second guessing any important decisions they make, and it's part of your task to help get them through that phase.
- Help them manage any significant changes that occur as a result of entering a relationship with you.
- Continue to call or write messages that show your personal interest in them and their success. Some of these contacts could be tied to birthdays or as follow-ups to personal interests.

Everybody feels some anxiousness after making important decisions, but Amiables are most likely to fret seriously after deciding. During the Closure stage, stick to what they value: Stay in contact, provide plenty of positive feedback, keep all the key players involved in the process, and make it feel personal.

ADAPTING YOUR STYLE FOR AMIABLES

As you now know, Amiables are ask-directed on the assertiveness scale and people-directed on the responsiveness scale. In adapting your behavior to make them comfortable with you, think about the behaviors that demonstrate warmth, patience and persistence.

As you learned with Analyticals, the central theme in increasing ask-directedness is relatively simple in theory: Ask more, tell less. Amiables don't want to be rushed on their decision-making, and they don't want to feel as if you are pushing them into uncharted territory.

As always, you have to complete the business at the core of your relationship, but proceed with patience and plenty of personal touches with Amiables or resistance and relationship tension are likely to increase. Therefore, with Amiables:

- *Ask for the opinions of others.* Make a point of asking plenty of questions. Let Amiables and other stakeholders in the process express their ideas. The most productive thing you can do with Amiables

Checklist for Adapting Behaviors toward Amiables

Try . . .	Avoid . . .
Breaking the ice with at least a brief personal comment.	Rushing immediately to get into your business or address the agenda.
Finding areas of common interest as a way of showing sincere interest on a personal level.	Sticking coldly to business, but also avoid getting so personal that you lose sight of your business goals.
Being candid and open.	Having hidden agendas and appearing as if you are manipulating things.
Talking about personal goals – listening and responding with focused attention.	Forcing the conversation toward quick decisions related to your objectives.
Presenting your case in a way that highlights people-related issues.	Overusing facts and figures to support your case.
Asking "why" questions to draw out their opinions.	Being demanding or threatening with position power.
Watching for early signs of disagreement or dissatisfaction.	Manipulating them into agreements because they won't "fight back."
Clearly defining – in writing – individual roles, responsibilities, and contributions.	Being vague or offering multiple options or probabilities.
Guaranteeing minimal risks, total satisfaction, and plenty of payoffs.	Making promises you can't keep; leaving them without ongoing support.

is to ask questions aimed at understanding their needs and helping them to get a clear picture of how you can help deal with them.

- *Negotiate decision-making.* It's not enough to let Amiables have their say. When they raise a point or offer a challenge, they're really looking for a chance to discuss their ideas and feelings from a personal perspective. Listen and respond to the feelings as well as the facts. It's vital to good communication with Amiables to acknowledge and value their views and expertise.

- *Listen without interrupting.* Patience is important. Like Analyticals, Amiables have a slower pace than Expressives or Drivers. Amiables also value a supportive environment. If you interrupt, or in other ways make them feel rushed, they may very likely take it personally. Amiables will also be concerned with others' reactions, or with the effects of actions on others, and they will need to voice these concerns. Don't interrupt or dismiss these points, even if they seem irrelevant to the task at hand at the time. Amiables need to be heard.

- *Adjust to the time needs of others.* A good sense of timing is as important as a sense of urgency. Be sensitive to the fact that some Amiables may want a fair amount of time to evaluate an idea and think it through completely. They may also want to confer with others. Provide them that opportunity.

- *Allow others to assume leadership roles.* You have to take charge when you are trying to build relationships, but Amiables work best in environments of shared leadership. Let your Amiables help create the agendas for your discussions, and provide sufficient opportunities for them to guide your conversations with their questions.

Comfort for Amiables also comes in working with people who can adapt to their people-directed behavior tendencies. The main thing to remember with Amiables (as it is with Expressives, who are the other people-directed Social Styles group) is that they are looking for warmth, personal connections, and attention in their relationships.

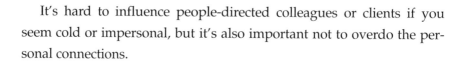

It's hard to influence people-directed colleagues or clients if you seem cold or impersonal, but it's also important not to overdo the personal connections.

UNDERSTANDING AND HANDLING BACK-UP BEHAVIOR WITH AMIABLES

The initial Back-Up Behavior of Amiables is called Acquiescing. They manage stress and tension in their relationships by limiting their exposure to the cause of their woes. They opt to surrender or give up, which is their way of taking flight from the situation.

In negotiating a tough decision about a new marketing strategy, for example, that means an unhappy Amiable may still meet with you to discuss the options you're debating, but your chances of winning agreement are slim. Amiables in this stage of Back-Up may respond positively to you during these discussions, even if they have already decided not to agree with your recommendations.

They might even go so far as to concur with you in a meeting to avoid creating new tension, and then retract the agreement later. Their ask-assertive and people-directed nature creates two important points about Amiables in Back-Up. First, because of their ask-assertive tendencies, you might not notice they have entered Back-Up. All of a sudden they start agreeing with you, not showing tension in their actions or body language. But, because of their people-directed responsiveness, they take conflict personally. If you keep Amiables in Back-Up too long (and when you don't sense they are in Back-Up, that is quite possible), you may never regain their trust.

Because Drivers and Expressives tend to fight in Back-Up, you might feel that the worst you can do is to upset an Expressive or Driver. But the truth is, an Amiable in Back-Up presents a tougher relationship to repair. An Expressive may explode in front of you, but will be more likely to forgive and forget. Amiables will tend not to forget, and if pushed far enough, will not forgive, ever!

The message you'll get from an Amiable who is Acquiescing is, "I give up. We will do it your way . . . until I get the chance to do it my way." That way begins the first moment you are out of sight.

If you reach this point but still want to try to salvage the relationship, step one is to refer back to the Listen-Share-Clarify-Problem Solve-Ask for Action (LSCPA) tool described Chapter 10 and work to *intervene* and reduce the Amiable's tension.

Determine what you need to do to begin your recovery. It's helpful to remember that, in most situations, Amiables are eager to develop solid, collaborative, personal relationships. Do whatever you can to reconnect to that core value and you will be on your way to resolving a tough situation. Getting through a crisis with an Amiable can actually enrich your long-term relationship.

IF YOU ARE AN AMIABLE

If you are an Amiable, you may be learning more details about Social Styles than you ever imagined you might need. After all, much of what we recommend about building productive relationships comes naturally to you, and relationships are among the most valued assets of your life. It's important for you to acknowledge, however, that some of your relationships are easier to manage than others, and it will be up to you to increase your Versatility to improve those that are not going as well as you would like.

It's unlikely the Drivers you know will ever have as much patience as you when it comes to decision-making. And, although the Analyticals you know are also inclined to be careful not to rush into things, they probably will rarely agree that your concerns about group consensus and the involvement of others should take precedence over bottom-line concerns. The Expressives in your life value relationships, too, but will often be pushing you to take some risks and to occasionally take a stance on an important issue – on your own.

Joyce Jappelle, an Amiable, has been diligent about being versatile for 15 years, ever since becoming part of the Wilson Learning Extended Enterprise.

Strengths, Weaknesses and Misperceptions – Amiables

Every Social Style has its strengths and weaknesses.

Strengths	Weaknesses
They have natural skills for coaching, counseling, and being helpful to others.	They can appear overly sensitive.
They provide support and positive strokes for other people's work and accomplishments.	They sometimes react too emotionally.
They have a sense of loyalty and dedication to those in their work and peer groups.	They may belabor decision-making to the point of being unable to make decisions at all.
They are willing to communicate that they value having trust and confidence in other people.	They can emphasize relationships to the point it may be perceived as interfering with tasks or deadlines.

Common Misperceptions about Amiables

Some common misperceptions about Amiables are that they place too much emphasis on relationships, move too slowly on important decisions and actions, and don't get results. Just as in every Social Style group, we all know of examples of Amiables who carry their strengths to excess and end up with counterproductive results. We all also know Amiables, however, who are successful and productive by all standard measures.

"One thing I learned quickly about Versatility is that there are lots of little things I can do to make other people comfortable. I realized how impatient I could sometimes get when I worked with Analyticals. Sometimes I got bored with all the details they would talk about. They tend to provide too much information for me. I realized that being detailed helps them to make decisions with comfort and confidence.

"I started using self-talk to remedy this problem. I knew that to have better relationships with Analyticals I had to pay more attention to the details, so I became conscious of doing that and saying to myself, 'This is my gift to the relationship.'

"I have also learned to be more versatile with Expressives. In many social situations I am essentially a shy person, so when someone gets excited about something and talks and talks and talks, I feel overwhelmed. To deal with this challenge, I can usually find a way to ask a question to bring people to a place where we can focus on one thing at a time." (Notice Joyce's natural ask-assertive behavior here?)

Joyce has also found it important, when working with groups of various styles, to make it clear she has something to offer for everybody.

"If I'm making a presentation to a group about how I do business, I'll let them know that I take a collaborative approach when appropriate, which appeals to other Amiables. I'll mention that I'll do a needs analysis to gather the data to assist in decision-making, which appeals to Analyticals. I'll point out that I will focus on using time well and use a results-oriented methodology, which addresses the concerns of Drivers. And I'll confirm that I'll operate in a way that fits with their big picture objectives, work with them to generate new ideas, and strive for doing things in a unique way, which takes into account the comfort of the Expressives in the group."

The lessons Joyce has learned fit well with the general advice about what Amiables can do to increase their Versatility:

- Take initiative and express a sense of urgency when appropriate.
- Assert yourself about your ideas on important issues.
- Be more sensitive to the time issues of other people.
- Contribute more of your ideas and opinions when the opportunity exists.
- Take action more readily and with a little less caution.

SUMMARY

- Amiables are ask- and people-directed. They are quiet, warm, easygoing, open, like sharing responsibility and consensus, seek approval or agreement, and are sometimes misperceived as putting too much emphasis on relationships and moving too slowly toward results.

- They expect you to build a relationship before starting to do business, and appreciate friendly, honest input. They want personal support, guarantees and assurances to limit risk.

- In Entry, the trust- and comfort-building stage, they won't focus on deadlines and results immediately. Keep a relaxed pace, mention mutual acquaintances, and stress reliability and proven success, not revolutionary ideas.

- In Dialogue, the problem-defining stage, listen responsively and create a cooperative tone. Ask about long-term goals and financial issues.

- In the Closure phase, when you are moving Amiables toward decisions about you and your ideas, expect them to draw in others and seek their satisfaction. Use past experiences, guarantees, and assurances. Avoid pressing hard.

- Help Amiables get support from other key stakeholders, watch for signs of second-guessing related to agreements you have made, handle details, and provide progress reports. Work out problems pleasantly.

- Amiables in Back-Up adopt Acquiescing behavior, a flight response. You may not notice it because it's not openly tense, but it's dangerous because they take conflict personally. If trust is lost, it may be irrecoverable. Try to reconnect to the core value of your relationship and intervene early.

- Amiables can improve their Versatility by taking more initiative, considering time and money issues more readily, voicing their opinions and ideas, and taking actions with a bit less caution than they normally would.

16 | Living and Working with Expressives

Being on the tightrope is living; everything else is waiting.
KARL WALLENDA

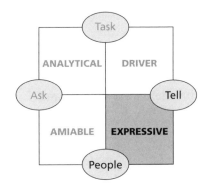

Living and working with Expressives can sometimes feel as if you are going through life holding the tail of comet. Expressives bring a lot of energy to their work and are eager and effective in sharing their ideas and getting people around them involved to make things happen. They are inspiring, emotional, and ultimately biased toward grandscale objectives. They move fast, but work hard to bring others along for the ride.

It doesn't take much to get an Expressive revved up about sharing ideas and dreams. They love to brainstorm and build on other people's insights.

Expressives fall on the same side of the assertiveness scale as Drivers; they are tell-directed. But they are more like Amiables on the responsiveness scale, tending to focus with greater interest on the people involved in a task than the task itself. They are comfortable taking the lead in social situations, and are willing to invest time and energy into conversation before feeling compelled to move on to tackling the task at hand. And intuition plays a major role in decision-making by Expressives. They tend to act on what "feels right."

Some of the phrases that will come to mind when you are working with Expressives are:

- Excitable, talkative and intuitive.
- Likes an audience, a bit of applause and general recognition.
- Risk-taker, competitive and spirited.
- Visionary, creative and inspirational.

As is the case with all Social Styles, Expressives bring many strengths to their work, including:

- An ability to energize and inspire others.
- A willingness and ability to stimulate the creative exchange of ideas.
- Enthusiasm and ambition.
- An ability to stretch people's thinking with their own dreams and far-reaching ideas.

Expressives are often misperceived as being too flighty, spending too much time building relationships and telling stories at the expense of being business-like and task oriented.

Expressives make for lively, challenging people to work with. Their quickness can make Analyticals and Amiables feel off balance and decidedly plodding. Their involvement with people can frustrate Drivers, who want to get on task faster. Expressives act with passion, intuition, creativity and influence. When it comes to collaboration, Expressives can be powerful allies if they believe in you and what you bring to a relationship.

EXPRESSIVE EXPECTATIONS

Break out your best listening skills, and maybe even your most comfortable shoes, when it comes to getting involved with Expressives.

The Expressive Style

Energetic. Inspiring. Emotional. Fast paced. Comfortable taking social initiative. Engages freely in friendly conversation before tackling tasks. Futuristic. Talkative. Intuitive. Willingly shares ideas, insights, dreams and visions. Risk-taker. Competitive. Spirited. Creative. Enthusiastic. Likes an audience. Ambitious.

Verbal and Nonverbal Cues	Energetic and enthusiastic. Gestures that are open and wide. Voice that is loud and varied. Fast-paced and lively.
Work Style	With others.
Attitude about Time	"Move fast, but spend time energizing others, sharing visions, dreams and ideas."
Attitude about Accomplishment	"Get results through people."
Attitude about Others	"It is very important to work with people to help make their own dreams reality."
Natural Work Activity Strengths	Motivating and reinforcing.
Personal Motivator	Recognition: Seeks to be highly visible and to stand out from the crowd, to be seen as unique and showing leadership. Values recognition for accomplishment, publicity, symbols of accomplishment.
Common Misperceptions about Expressives	Flighty, more inclined to tell a joke than discuss a business issue. Not businesslike or task-oriented.

They are quick to speak, somewhat reluctant to give up the floor when they are engaged in conversation, and, when they are going full speed, not much inclined to listen – except perhaps to hear their own ideas confirmed.

You might also want to make sure you have an easy-to-read road map in mind for finding your way back from conversations that can take unexpected twists and turns. Every bend in your discussion with an Expressive matters, although at times it may seem as if they are expecting quite a bit of you to be able to keep up with their sweeping and far-reaching views of the world.

The comfortable shoes will come in handy if you happen to be standing, say, by the water cooler or the company coffee pot when your conversation begins. It could last a while.

Expressives expect you to:

- *Develop your relationship openly.* Expressives like to operate in a friendly, inclusive atmosphere.
- *Be tolerant of their casual use of time.* Expressives sometimes seem to deliberately cultivate a casual, relaxed approach without much regard for time. That often changes, however, when they are driving toward a goal. They don't worry much about the clock, until they have made a decision about what they want. At that point, they want rapid results.
- *Present the "big picture" first.* Expressives want to discuss and grasp the overall view of a situation before getting into the details.
- *Collaborate.* Expressives want you to work *with* them on proposing what will best serve them, their teams, their organizations. They thrive on the exchange of ideas.
- *Help them get a clear sense of who you are and how you communicate, relate, and operate.* Expressives appreciate dealing with people who are competent and confident. They will be impressed by solid experience and references and testimonials from other people with whom you have had similar relationships.
- *Share sincere thoughts and feelings openly with them.* Expressives recognize others as being integral to reaching their goals, but they also value people as individuals. They want to get to know you on a more personal level.

- *Provide them with recognition for their visions and actions.* Expressives want support for their ideas and decisions and will look to you for positive reinforcement. If you provide that support, it will add to an Expressive's perceived value of your relationship. In business, Expressives want to like the people with whom they interact, and will be encouraged and pleased by your efforts to build a personal relationship.
- *Assure them you value and will implement their ideas.* Expressives want to be confident in the quality of work done and will be comforted when they see their passion and thinking translated into actions you can complete on their behalf or in their interest.

ENTRY WITH EXPRESSIVES

Lack of trust, as we have repeatedly emphasized, is the number-one obstacle to effective communication and productive relationships. The number-one strategy for contending with lack of trust is to do whatever you can, as soon as you can, to build credibility.

Even though Expressives tend to ignore the passage of time when they are initiating relationships, it is important for you to be fast paced in establishing who you are, what you have to offer, and what the Expressives have to gain by welcoming you into a relationship.

In the Entry stage with Expressives:

- Quickly describe the purpose for your contact, whether it's a phone call, letter or face-to-face encounter. You are going to have to earn the right to develop a relationship with Expressives.
- Share stories about people you both know.
- Share information that would be perceived as "exclusive."
- Share your feelings and enthusiasm for the ideas of Expressives.
- Once you have established your competence and feel you have earned some initial confidence with Expressives, take some time to open up the relationship on a more personal level.
- Reinforce Expressives for their energy, vision and enthusiasm.

When making your Purpose, Process and Payoff statements with Expressives, be open, friendly, and quick to emphasize the benefits they will experience by trusting you and what you bring to the relationship. When talking about your reasons for being together, tie into the "big picture" first and foremost whenever you can, and keep the conversation about the details brief. Promise the process will be quick and inclusive, and as much as possible hook the outcomes of your discussions, plans, and work to the dreams you know the Expressive wants to fulfill.

DIALOGUE WITH EXPRESSIVES

Unlike when dealing to Drivers, it won't take much effort to get Expressives talking about their needs and ideas. That's helpful because Dialogue is critical to building a foundation for any relationship.

Your goal in the Dialogue stage is to get clear what is important to others. Uncover their problems. Learn their priorities. Understand the role they play in the community you share and the forces that are influencing their thinking and actions. Determine where you might fit in that world, and begin to make the case about why this person should be open to letting that happen.

Remember to turn back to the Dialogue section of Chapter 11 to refresh yourself in the kinds of questions you can use in this stage of your relation-building process (permission questions, fact-finding questions, feeling-finding questions, best-least questions, and magic-wand questions). But, if you can strike the right chord with Expressives in the Entry stage, you will have earned the right to hear what's on their minds, so it will be extremely important to be ready to listen and to use questions selectively to make sure you cover all the vital areas you need to understand.

In the Dialogue stage with Expressives:

• Begin by asking about their vision of outcomes that are integral to your relationship.

- Identify other people who should be involved in or will be influenced by the relationship.
- Listen, then respond with plenty of verbal and non-verbal feedback that supports their beliefs.
- Keep the discussion fast paced, focused, moving toward a result.
- Question carefully for the data you need. One challenge may be finding openings in an Expressive's side of the conversation where you can slip in inquiries. Be patient and alert.
- When the interest in the specifics of what you are talking about wanes, summarize what has been discussed and begin to suggest ways to move to the next steps.

Expressives have a number of strengths that are often helpful in building a relationship. They are typically open to sharing whatever information they believe you need to understand them and their situation. They will collaborate, even in the preliminary planning stages, on projects you may be initiating or issues you are promoting that will eventually affect them. Expressives will show their concerns about the quality of your joint efforts as well as for the action steps you undertake, so there will be few mysteries about how they are feeling. When necessary, Expressives will also adapt to the needs of others, and they are willing to innovate and take risks.

All of these tendencies can be beneficial in your efforts to help Expressives get whatever support or assurance they might need in order to feel comfortable as they move their relationships forward with you. Look for opportunities to engage an Expressive's strengths as fully as possible.

Establishing your credibility (as described in Chapter 11) with Expressives will also be different from what you do with the other styles:

- As described in Chapter 11, you will need to establish your credibility. They way you do that with Expressives is somewhat different than with people of other styles.

- *Propriety:* While Expressives, like everyone else, expect you to adhere to appropriate business expectations around customs and appearance, a little added flair will catch the Expressive's eye and enhance your credibility. To Expressives, adding that colorful tie or scarf to your normal business suit is a way of saying that you are confident in yourself and are willing to put yourself a bit on display.
- *Competence:* Success stories and testimonials from others who can speak to your competence are what Expressives look for. For Expressives, testamonials are best when they come from people they admire, whether from personal experience or by reputation. If you have completed a similar project, for example, with a highly respected person or company, that success story will communicate a lot for an Expressive.
- *Commonality.* Sharing commonality of interests and experiences with Expressives is important in establishing credibility. Your shared excitement and love of challenge is communicated through your shared interests.
- *Intent.* For Expressives, communicating positive intent, but without expressing passion for that intent, is like not communicating intent at all. Expressives will not only want to know your intent, but will want to know that you stand behind your intent with excitement and passion.

CLOSURE WITH EXPRESSIVES

If you are able to maintain Expressives' comfort through the Entry and Dialogue stages, you are in good position to begin the Closure phase – to start moving them toward decisions, action plans, and a commitment to a relationship with you. You are ready to present your ideas, ask for agreements related to specific projects or tasks, and deal with any resistance that might exist.

Affirming

Your challenge with Expressives is to understand and agree upon the "big picture" to the point that you have earned enough trust and confidence to solidify your relationship. As always, don't lose track of the details. Come back to them when you have locked in the commitment to act.

- Provide ideas in writing. Take care to make sure your thinking and recommendations reflect the ideas of Expressives, using their vocabulary, examples, etc. Build confidence that you understand their desires and have the necessary facts to understand their needs and interests, but don't overwhelm them with details.
- When you are at the point in your relationship with an Expressive that you are looking for a commitment to action, if you have enough information to have tested the appropriateness of your recommendations thoroughly in your own mind, assume the decision is made. Ask, in a casual, informal way, for the Expressive to move forward with you.
- Work to get final commitments to action in writing and make sure everybody is clear about what has been agreed upon.
- Save the details about your agreements until you have a firm commitment to go ahead with a plan. Expressives will be looking for you to handle the fine points of the project.
- Don't confuse things by offering options.
- Don't leave decisions vague or unclear.
- Don't be curt or reserved.

As with Drivers, Expressives will ultimately hold you accountable for knowing all the details for whatever plans you agree to implement. It can be counterproductive, however, to spend time in the Closure stage to present excessive facts, figures, alternatives and abstractions.

Supporting

It is important in the Closure stage with Expressives, as it is with all Social Styles, to behave in ways that show your ongoing interest in supporting, preserving and growing your relationship. This phase is especially important with Expressives because they are perhaps most likely to voluntarily spread good news about you if they are impressed with what you do with and for them. That can open doors for many other potentially important relationships for you.

- Provide testimonials from people Expressives see as important or prominent.
- Don't rush the discussion. Spend time engaging Expressives in developing ways to implement your plan.
- Manage schedules carefully.
- Personally introduce any other individuals whom you bring into the Expressive's own circle of acquaintances because of your relationship.
- Help get the details sorted, organized and well in hand to serve whatever purpose will be required by an Expressive.
- Be proactive and personal in resolving any problems. Look for ways to make things easier for Expressives.

Enhancing

- When the opportunity presents itself, offer something value-added or unique. This can be part of making Expressives feel special.
- Find a way to highlight the personal aspects of the relationship you have developed.
- Always express your desire to stay close to an Expressive, even if your agreements and collaboration put layers of other people between you to complete certain tasks. Maintain a personal connection and responsibility for the relationship and what it entails.
- In a professional situation, take an Expressive's lead in planning social or informal contacts. If he or she suggests lunch or dinner meetings, use these as opportunities to develop the relationship further.
- Inform Expressives of new, different, breakthrough things in your life that may be of influence or interest in theirs.

- Appeal to personal esteem needs. Help Expressives feel special in your dealings with them.
- Celebrate. Take time to recognize completion and success with Expressives. Expressives, more than other Social Styles, value the more tangible representations of a successfully completed project. Mementoes, personalized cards and small gifts to symbolize the success and the relationship can count for a lot.

Expressives tend to be futuristic and holistic in their thinking. The Closure stage is the time when you want to be asking and thinking about, "What's next?" If you meet or exceed expectations with Expressives, they are going to want to talk about that success and be in the frame of mind to expand their ideas about what else they can do with you to be successful.

ADAPTING YOUR STYLE FOR EXPRESSIVES

Comfort for Expressives comes from working with people who can adapt to their tell-directed, people-directed behavior tendencies. On the people-directed side of that equation, the main thing to remember with Expressives (and Amiables, who are the other people-directed Social Styles group) is that they are looking for a little warmth in their relationships.

It is difficult to influence people-directed customers if you come across as cold or impersonal, but it's also important not to overdo the personal connections. Some restraint in the way you express your feelings will reflect your ability to handle feelings in a mature, professional manner. Being too reserved or focusing excessively on the facts, however, can make you appear unwilling or unable to understand the emotional issues that are important to Expressives and influence their decisions. To help personalize your contacts with Expressives:

- *Verbalize your feelings*. Talk openly about how you feel about the issues you're handling with Expressives. You can establish better rela-

Checklist for Modifying Behaviors toward Expressives

Try . . .	Avoid . . .
Planning interaction that supports their dreams and intentions.	Addressing the logic, feasibility, or practical implementation of their ideas.
Leaving time for relating and socializing.	Being curt, cold or reserved.
Talking about their goals and other people's ideas they find stimulating.	Presenting facts and figures, alternatives and abstractions.
Providing few details and instead suggesting ways to achieve their goals.	Contradicting their vision or not implementing their decisions.
Asking for their opinions and ideas about people.	Wasting time being impersonal or judgmental.
Taking enough time to discuss their ideas and views.	Kidding around too much, or "sticking to the agenda" too diligently.
Providing testimonials from people they consider prominent and important.	Talking down to them or providing too much detail.
Offering special, immediate, and personal incentives.	Being dogmatic or prescriptive.
Supporting the individual and her ideas.	Supporting just the facts.

tionships by acknowledging your honest reactions. If you are upset, let that be known. Likewise, let it show when you are enthusiastic or excited about where you are headed.

- *Pay personal compliments.* Sincere, legitimate compliments are always welcome by Expressives. Don't hesitate to express these kinds of positive sentiments, or to find other more indirect ways to say good things about them. For example, remember their birthdays, write them personal notes, or inquire about family members or the important things they do outside of their professional lives.
- *Be willing to spend time on personal relationships.* Learn to pay attention to the feeling side of human nature. You may not always see an

immediate, direct connection between personal involvement with Expressives and achieving business goals, for example, but friendship and sensitivity to the feelings of others can enrich relationships and build feelings of loyalty and cooperation with Expressives. It can pay off to let your personal feelings enter into a professional relationship in a balanced, appropriate way.

- *Make small talk. Socialize.* Expressives don't want all their communication with you to be "strictly business." Always keep your conversations ultimately focused on your strategic goals and objectives, but mix in bits of conversation that have nothing to do with business.

Expressives are also tell-directed on the assertiveness scale. The strategy for modifying your behavior to accommodate this preference: Ask fewer questions and provide more answers. Tell more often.

UNDERSTANDING AND HANDLING BACK-UP BEHAVIOR WITH EXPRESSIVES

The first instinct for Expressives feeling tense about a relationship gone wrong is to fight. When they reach the point of Back-Up, it first shows as Attacking Behaviors.

Expressives in Back-Up manage their tension by trying to control the situation using emotions and feelings – their strengths – but with a negative, discomforting slant. Their interest in creating excitement with people can change into a personal and public attack. Their affinity for making others feel good can shift into an unsettling ability to make others feel at fault. And their natural preference to reinforce others when things are going well can become an uncanny talent for probing others' vulnerabilities.

An Expressive in Back-Up is thinking, "You and your ideas are *ridiculous*. What are you thinking? What was *I* thinking when I let this relationship get this far?"

The sooner you begin to *neutralize* Expressives in Back-Up by letting them vent, of course, the more likely you are to be able to recover the relationship. To adapt the **Listen-Share-Clarify-Problem-Solve Ask for Action (LSCPA)** tool for this purpose, refer back to Chapter 10.

Remember, although angry Expressives will at times be unwilling to talk or to share their feelings, tell-directed, people-directed people ultimately want to connect with you on a personal level. They want to speak, and they want you to listen – closely.

IF YOU ARE AN EXPRESSIVE

If you are an Expressive, take a deep breath. Pause for a moment of silence and give some quiet thought to the impact your enthusiasm may sometimes have on people who don't have quite the same energy as you on certain topics.

One the biggest mistakes Marilyn Smith ever made using – or not using – Social Styles was interpreting a potential client's initial enthusiastic response to a phone call as an indicator she was an Expressive, like Marilyn herself.

Marilyn, who teaches Social Styles for Wilson Learning, says she jumped to a conclusion about this person, and then, feeling very comfortable about dealing with someone of the same Social Style, went about trying to sell to her in her own enthusiastic, high-energy manner.

"We had a very difficult relationship for months. I was frustrated I couldn't get any information from her. And she always seemed so impatient with me. I felt I had no credibility with her. It finally occurred to me, based on a series of difficult conversations, I needed to reassess my thoughts about her Social Style. I concluded she was probably an Analytical and revised my strategy for working with her.

"It worked. The more information I gave to her up front, and the more task-responsive I was, the better she responded to me. In the end, we not only forged a comfortable business relationship, but also a strong personal connection."

Sherry Schoolcraft has also learned firsthand about the importance of knowing when it can be helpful to tone down her Expressive characteristics.

Strengths, Weaknesses and Misperceptions – Expressives

Every Social Style has its strengths and weaknesses.

Strengths	Weaknesses
They create excitement, involvement.	They can be overly excitable.
They share visions and ideas.	They can be futuristic to the point of not being pragmatic.
They motivate and inspire others.	They can be impulsive.
They are open about their feelings.	They can sometimes overlook facts and be overly dependent on feelings and intuition.
They make others feel good about themselves because they are valued.	They can lose track of important details.
They have a natural tendency to reinforce others.	

Common Misperceptions about Expressives

Common misperceptions about Expressives are that they are flighty, more inclined to tell a joke than to focus on a business issue, and not business-like or task oriented. The reality is that Expressives who are motivated, challenged and excited are effective at achieving their goals.

"When I teach Social Styles to people, I get Social Style profiles of all the participants in advance of each class. I know that one of the first things I have to consider is what that information tells me about the make-up of the group. Based on what I see about the mix of styles in the group, I plan whether I'm going to have to teach in a style that keeps the class hopping along to make the Drivers comfortable. . . allow time for the thoughtful questions Analyticals and Amiables are going to want to ask. . . plan some story-telling exercise for the Expressives. . . and I think about whether as an Expressive myself, I'll need to limit some of my hand gestures and facial expressions.

"Before I understood Social Styles, I wouldn't have been conscious of the pace of my teaching or my body language. I would have just gone in and conducted myself in the way I always conducted myself. And things probably wouldn't have gone so well."

This awareness of Social Styles has also paid off for Sherry in sales situations. Early in her Wilson Learning career, she made a joint sales visit along with an Expressive salesperson not well-versed in Social Styles and "watched her expressiveness bounce off the walls."

The Analytical decision-makers in the room were retreating in the face of this display, she says, and it was only by pulling back and toning down, referring to facts and making time for detailed questions, that they were able to salvage the sale.

It pays to pay attention, say Sherry and Marilyn. The big picture for Expressives who want to increase Versatility:

- Pay attention to the details supplied by others.
- Keep your emotions open, but under control.
- Acknowledge the ideas of others.
- Allow time for others to move at a comfortable pace.
- Restrain your enthusiasm.
- Guard against being impulsive.
- Talk less and listen more.
- Make decisions based on facts.
- Organize your thoughts in logical patterns.

SUMMARY

- Expressives are tell- and people-directed. They are energetic, intuitive, talkative, enthusiastic, ambitious risk-takers. They move fast, energize others, appreciate recognition and visibility, and are misperceived as flighty and not businesslike or task-oriented.

- They expect you to listen, be open, be flexible about time, think of the "big picture," collaborate, and they like it when you value their ideas.
- In Entry, the trust-building stage, quickly earn credibility with stories of mutual acquaintances, exclusive information, shared feelings, and endorsement for their energy and vision.
- During Dialogue, the problem-defining stage, use your questioning skills to define the goals and the problems you will tackle together. Innovation and risk-taking may very likely be part of what you need to undertake together.
- In the Closure phase, when you are moving people toward accepting you and your ideas, use Expressives' own words and thoughts. Make them feel special and appreciated. Don't drown them in detail or options, and don't rush the discussion or act reserved.
- During Closure, take lots of personal responsibility and handle details of the relationship yourself. Celebrate, look to future successes, and expand the scope of your work together.
- Expressives in Back-Up adopt Attacking behavior, the fight response. They try to control the situation with feelings. Neutralize tension by drawing feelings out fully before rectifying the situation.
- If you are an Expressive, at times you must tone down your enthusiasm and allow others to inject their thoughts, ideas, and decisions.

LESSONS FROM SOCIAL STYLES EXPERTS

17 | Speeding Up the Learning Curve

Good judgment comes from experience, and a lot of that comes from bad judgment.

WILL ROGERS

You're ready. If you haven't been using some of what you've learned about Social Styles through the first 16 chapters, it's time to start. But be prepared to make a few mistakes, stumble, and find yourself at times slightly confused and flustered.

It's going to take practice to become comfortable using the Social Styles tools and concepts. However, even when you identify styles incorrectly, you're better off than if you make no effort at all to understand what people's behaviors can tell you about their style and what you can do to make them comfortable in relationships.

Even if you do guess wrong about a person's Social Style, your adjustments to your own behavior may still pay off. If you mistake an Expressive for a Driver, for example, you will still be right in adjusting your behavior to be more tell-assertive, since both Expressives and Drivers are tell-assertive. However, when you adjust your behavior to be more task-responsive, which is appropriate for a Driver, you'll see that your Expressive won't feel comfortable, since an Expressive is people-responsive, not task-responsive. Then you'll realize you are in fact dealing with an Expressive, and you'll start to emphasize people first – and notice the impact on the person.

This cycle is just what we described in Chapter 5. You observe behavior, you decide how to act (adjusting your behavior), and then you watch the results and fine-tune your behavior accordingly. So even if you guess wrong, 75 percent of the time your guess will give you at least partially positive results. Only when you guess a style that is diagonally opposite the person's true style will you be 100 percent wrong. And you'll probably immediately notice your adjustments aren't working and correct them (see the Appendix for tips).

As you practice you will get better, and learn some important lessons from personal experience. To speed up the learning curve for you, here are some lessons others have learned over the past four decades.

TAKE IT SLOWLY

"It's too easy to make snap judgments about Social Styles," says Bob Davis, a senior associate with McCourt Associates in Nahant, Massachusetts in the US. "Slow down. Don't base things on a single word or behavior. Drivers can use the word 'love.' Amiables sometimes say, 'Just do it!' Analyticals can say, 'Whoa, baby!' And Expressives can say, 'I need more details.'

"Use multiple clues to identify people's styles. Pay attention to what people say, how they say it, how they animate or don't animate their expressions. You need to look at clusters of behavior. If monitors were to follow a group of us around for a day putting dots on a Social Styles matrix for each behavior they observed, they would be putting dots in every quadrant for every one of us. At the end of the day, however, one quadrant for each of us would like it had been hit with birdshot. There would be one quadrant with the biggest cluster of behaviors. That would be home."

Hans Fenner, founder of Capita-Consulting in Stuttgart, Germany, agrees that acting too early on assumptions in new relationships increases the chances of behaving outside others' comfort zones. "Ask enough questions so that you can really discover somebody's needs. Sometimes people are forced to behave contrary to their individual preferences because of business needs. For example, an Amiable customer may not like to bargain, but may have to negotiate fiercely because of the company's need to save money."

That single behavior in the example Hans uses might tell you that you're dealing with a Driver, but you would probably quickly find yourself on the wrong course in this relationship.

One of the keys to mastering Social Styles is to use it every day, says James Miller, the software development manager for Qwest in Denver, Colorado in the US..

"Put it into practice in every part of your life. The good news is that it's easy to do that. And it's effective. I was thrilled to figure out that I would be able to apply Social Styles to my personal life even though I learned about it in the context of my work. I think I've done a better job of raising my daughter and getting along with my wife because of these concepts.

"You can't change who you are, but you can improve your Versatility. I'm a Driver. There's a joke at my house when we have to make decisions. My wife asks, 'What shall we do?' I say, 'You know me, Mr. Flexible. It doesn't matter, whatever we decide.'" This kind of awareness really helps when it comes to understanding relationships.

So, take it slow, but have a go. Bob Davis says, "Don't be afraid to try and fail. As Winston Churchill once said, 'Success is going from failure to failure with great enthusiasm.'"

DON'T JUMP TO CONCLUSIONS

It's also important not to make assumptions about the reasons for other people's behavior. For example, if the new manager in the marketing department wants to spend time to get to know you personally before digging into the details of a new campaign, don't assume he or she is not interested in the task or is wasting time.

STAY AWAY FROM STEREOTYPES

Not all Italians are Expressives. Not all women are Amiables. Not all CEOs are hard-edged, bottom-line Drivers who don't like puppies or children. The data we've collected about Social Styles for nearly 40 years shows that some industries, some professions, and some cultures do have slightly higher representation of certain styles. But pick a stereotype and we'll show countless examples of people who disprove it. Not even all accountants or engineers are Analyticals.

The Social Styles data apply worldwide. People of all nations split almost evenly over the four quadrants of the Social Styles matrix. It does help when you are working on international relationships, however, to be aware of cultural differences that provide varying behavioral clues.

BE REALISTIC ABOUT THE POWER OF SOCIAL STYLES

Some people want to be able to have Social Styles alone resolve every tough interpersonal issue in their lives, says Tevilla Riddell.

"Getting good at using Social Styles can have a tremendous impact, but it really can't answer every question about your relationships. It only deals with communication behavior. I had a woman in one of my workshops who said, 'I want to understand why I don't get along with my child.' I had another whose goal was to have Social Styles help her understand why her son skips classes at school. And I have had business leaders say they want to figure out why they can't get people to work harder."

The way Social Styles can help with challenges of this sort, she says, is in giving you tools to discuss what needs to be cleared up.

"Social Styles can help you through the conversations about tough issues. If you can't talk about a problem, you can't deal with it."

BE AWARE OF STYLES WITHIN STYLES

As we have pointed out before, there is a wide variation in how people communicate even within each of the four main styles. In fact, you will find a wide range of styles within each quadrant of the Social Styles matrix.

For example, you might have four co-workers who are all Drivers. In comparison to each other, however, one may be extremely tell-directed, even in comparison to the three other Drivers. Another may be significantly more ask-directed than the other three. The third might be obviously more task-directed than the others, and the fourth might be more people-directed than any of the others. Don't let the variations confuse you. They are all still Drivers – all considered to be tell-directed on the assertiveness scale and task-directed on the responsive scale. The full measure of your Versatility will be taken when you must adapt your behaviors to the finer points of distinguishing these kinds of subtleties.

ACCEPT PEOPLE'S BEHAVIOR AS A SIGN OF THEIR COMFORT ZONES AND NOTHING MORE

Remember that thoughts and feelings are not part of Social Style analysis. You are watching for observable behaviors that indicate comfort with a certain communication style, but that does not tell you what is going on in people's heads or hearts.

Don Luce of ELA, a San Francisco, California consultancy in the Wilson Learning network, once observed, "Sometimes the people you're closest to prove to be the hardest to type. That's precisely because you *do* know what they are thinking and feeling – at least some of the time. So you might think your sister is an Expressive because she shares her feelings so freely with you. Others would see how she prefers to get on top of tasks in almost all her other interactions, and type her correctly as a Driver."

Nevertheless, Marilyn Smith suggests that people who are learning about Social Styles start out practicing style analysis, adapting behavior, and observing the results first with family and friends. "They're more likely to be forgiving when we don't get it right. It takes time and practical experience to get comfortable with these new skills."

OBSERVE ONE DIMENSION OF BEHAVIOR – ASSERTIVENESS OR RESPONSIVENESS – AT A TIME

It's difficult to assess all behaviors and Social Style indicators at once. Break your observations into chunks. To evaluate on the assertiveness scale, ask, "Is this person more or less inclined to ask questions than I am when it comes to trying to influence people's thoughts and actions?" Your answer can locate someone to the left or right of the midpoint on the assertiveness scale, which narrows your decision to two choices. To the left, the person is either an Analytical or an Amiable. To the right, a Driver or an Expressive.

To evaluate someone on the responsiveness scale, ask, "When it comes to expressing feelings about a project, is this person more or less inclined than I am to focus on the people on a team?" Your response will locate a person above or below the midpoint on this scale. Again, this gives you two choices. Above the midpoint a person is more task-directed – an Analytical or a Driver. Below the midpoint, the focus is more people-directed – an Amiable or an Expressive.

OBSERVE VERBAL AND NONVERBAL BEHAVIORS – AND BE OBJECTIVE

If you tend to smile when meeting someone new, don't immediately assume that someone else who is serious-faced and stern-voiced is unhappy, unapproachable, or dislikes you. Use Social Styles to understand that this person may be a Driver or an Analytical who naturally prefers to be reserved initially, and remember what that implies about their communication preferences. Read the body language. Listen for word choice and voice inflection. Ask yourself, "What is this person telling me about the way he or she likes to interact?" This person may be looking for evidence of your experience or competence

167

before letting the relationship begin to develop. The smiles may come later.

Joyce Jappelle reminds us that it is important to pay attention not only to the verbal and nonverbal cues you get from others, but also to be mindful of what your own behaviors communicate about your Versatility. Joyce, president of Collaborative Change Systems in Denver, Colorado in the US, watched one of her potential business projects disappear because she misread the messages being communicated between her and the client.

"The client, who was clearly an Amiable, had been introduced to me through a referral. She asked me for a proposal to submit to her CEO. When I followed up after giving it to her she kept telling me everything was going well and she was getting everything she needed. She told me she preferred e-mail as a means of contact, which is unusual for an Amiable. After a long delay I finally heard that things were on hold and my client had not even submitted the proposal to her CEO. Clearly I had missed something. I hadn't developed enough trust with her so that she could tell me what had changed. And my behavior was hindering the relationship."

START ASSESSING STYLES EVEN BEFORE YOUR FIRST MEETING

You can use Social Styles to prepare for first contacts with people you don't know. Whether you are meeting the leader of a newly assembled cross-functional team or hiring a contractor to work on your house, you can talk to others who know these people and ask style-related questions – even if your source person doesn't know Social Styles.

Ask for descriptions about the person's habits and characteristics (e.g., Does she tend to speak fast or slowly? Does he use many gestures or facial expressions? Does she like to start meetings punctually and get right into the agenda? Will she want to see a lot of data to support recommendations?). One caveat: As you ask, keep in mind the style of the person sharing these insights. To an Expressive, another Expressive doesn't necessarily speak quickly. And the phrase "a lot of data" will mean something different to an Amiable than it does to an Analytical.

USE INTRODUCTIONS AS EARLY INDICATIONS OF STYLE

If you don't get enough information to pin down a specific Social Style before meeting, try at least to determine where the person lands on either the assertiveness or responsiveness scales.

Use your opening conversations as a safe and comfortable way to approach any of the four styles and begin your assessment. For example, simply ask, "How are you today?" and let the other person choose how far to carry that discussion. Where the conversation goes will begin to tell you about the person's level of people-directedness.

Tom Kramlinger, a business solution consultant for Wilson Learning based in Longwood, Florida in the US, describes these first moments in a personal encounter as a "style-free, business-free grace period." He believes it is available with people of all styles and in just about all situations.

"When meeting any new person, whether in business or otherwise, there is a period of standard chit-chat about background, weather, geography, and sports that takes place no matter what your style.

"I don't worry about misreading styles during that period. Nor do I expect to get a tremendous amount of insight into other people's styles. But it is a beginning. It is a ritual of acquaintance making. It's the time to focus on commonality – to get a sense of what we have in common that we can use to start a relationship. But as that part of a conversation starts to wind down, my Social Style antennae really go up. Who is continuing to talk? Are they trying to convince or just share? Are they focusing on the people or the task in the topic? Is their level of animation going up or starting to abate? That's when I start to adjust my style. The idea is to use the energy of the grace period to get an early read on the style dynamics."

A person's physical environment can also provide quick insights.

At Analyst International Corp., where James Miller was first trained in Social Styles, his job entailed managing field service consultants assigned to work full time at client locations. In addition to managing those relationships he also worked closely with the people in the client companies who supervised his team members on a daily basis.

"Social Styles was a real boon to me, especially when I had to facilitate putting people into new assignments. I would meet with the new client managers, and I knew the success of the assignments hinged in large part on those relationships."

James learned to go in cold to these meetings and to use the visual messages in people's offices to provide important Social Styles clues.

"I would step into a cubicle or an office and try to evaluate Social Style based on how the space was decorated. You get a feel when you walk in. I could be pretty sure if the client had a photo of a neighborhood block party prominent on the desk I was dealing with an Amiable. Charts and graphs and desks cluttered with files were a good sign that I was dealing with an Analytical. If I saw community service awards or signs of the person being in a community theater company, I suspected I was working with an Expressive."

Reading these kinds of signs, and quickly figuring out how to modify his behavior during these visits, James says, is how he honed his Social Styles skills.

FOCUS ON MAKING ONLY MINOR MODIFICATIONS IN YOUR BEHAVIOR

If there were a place over the rainbow called the Land of Analytical, or the Republic of Driver, you wouldn't need to speak fluent "Analyse" or "Driverese" to visit those worlds. But knowing some key phrases and customs of the native peoples would go a long way toward improving communication and making for a more pleasant and productive visit.

Derek O'Brien, Managing Director of Wilson Learning Ireland in Dublin, uses this line of thinking in talking about Versatility in his Social Styles workshops. The point, he says, is that minor – but strategic – changes in behavior, not major overhauls, are most effective in building productive relationships.

"Imagine what it would be like if people in each Social Style quadrant spoke a different language. It would be extremely difficult to communicate among the quadrants or styles. To communicate effectively you would need to add to your own natural language some of the phrases with which styles different from yours are comfortable. This wouldn't imply that you were suddenly a different person – a native speaker of any other language. Instead, you would be showing not only your awareness of the differences between yourself and others, but also that you are prepared to take the initiative to minimize problems that might be caused by these differences. Likewise, Versatility does not mean changing your style or who you are. It does mean adding behaviors with which other styles are comfortable to your own behavioral "vocabulary.""

LIVE BY THE PLATINUM RULE

The Golden Rule – "Do unto others as you would have them do unto you" – falls a bit short when you look at the world through the lens of Social Styles. What makes you comfortable can have the opposite effect on someone of a different style.

"I can't take credit for coining the phrase, but the better alternative is to live by The Platinum Rule – to communicate with people in the way in which they want be communicated with," says Sherry Schoolcraft from her perspective as a consultant in the Wilson Learning Extended Enterprise.

Larry Wilson, founder of Wilson Learning, puts his slant on The Platinum Rule this way: "Do unto others as they would have you do unto them. Everybody knows that ounce for ounce, platinum is worth more than gold," Larry says.

James Miller uses this platinum approach in his supervisory role at Qwest. "A fellow I used to work with taught me something I thought was a real revelation. He said a lot of folks who don't manage others in a workplace think you have to treat everybody the same to be fair. But you shouldn't. It is much more effective for me to treat people with respect to their own unique needs, wants, and preferences. It's like the old football coach who knows that some people need a hug and others a swift kick to be inspired to do their best. Knowing what people of different Social Styles need is the difference for me in being as good and effective a manager as I can be.

"I use Social Styles to determine how I can put people in situations where they can be most successful. Competition is tough. We all have to be very careful with our spending. My job is to put people in situations they can handle well and where they feel good about what they are doing."

Tom Kramlinger also uses the platinum approach in numerous ways, including preparing for contact with potential customers.

"Whenever I accompany a colleague to a meeting, for example, I always ask, 'What is the Social Style of the person we are meeting?' When I write a document, I want to know the styles of the audience for it so that I know how to organize it, how long to make it, what evidence to include, what tone to use, and what to emphasize.

"The essence of business is to exchange something with other people who are not necessarily your friends. Social Styles is an excellent way to establish a comfortable basis of communication so that the exchange goes smoothly."

VALUE DIVERSITY

Dan Gordon sees the Social Styles concepts as integral to building successful work teams, in large part because of the way this tool can be used to understand and build on the diverse strengths and attributes people of different styles bring to the workplace.

Dan is a senior technical manager at General Mills, a multinational food products company based in Minneapolis, Minnesota in the US. He has been involved in numerous start-up projects and many new-product introductions. He has also been involved in the merger of operations and cultures that resulted when General Mills acquired Pillsbury.

In response to that last challenge, Dan turned directly to Social Styles for help.

General Mills had conducted employee climate surveys and held focus groups with workers to give managers insights into areas needing development in the company. In part, that assessment showed people sensed a strong need to improve communication and teamwork – to create a climate of camaraderie and cooperation – in order to handle their daily business challenges most effectively.

"We were going through lots of change. We had new people come into our area from Pillsbury. We had new hires. We wanted to build a positive spirit, so we started looking for tools to use. I had taken a Social Styles class about 20 years before we started dealing with this merger, was still using the concepts, and believed they could help us."

So, Dan brought together his diverse group and used Social Styles to establish a working environment where everybody would be accepted without judgment. "There was no right or wrong style."

The payoff in valuing and accentuating the diversity within the team was immediate and significant, Dan says. "It was very helpful to get a clarifying sense of how peers viewed each other, and to understand how accepting and working with those differences could be beneficial for us.

"The investment in this experience has easily paid itself back a hundred-fold particularly in enabling our decision-making. People have learned to recognize situations when they need to appeal to different styles in order to get their points of view across. That awareness alone helps cut decision time and the need for follow-up meetings or for bringing in additional resources."

On another front, Dan says, taking advantage of the diversity of Social Styles in their teams helps them develop the best options for project plans or problems they encounter. "Each style brings a different perspective to the challenge. Having people with different Social

Styles working together ensures we are looking at a problem from all angles before making a final decision. This helps prevent us from being blindsided or from taking too narrow an approach."

Dan, who is an Analytical, also uses Social Style to make the most of diversity in his day-to-day management tasks.

"My style when I meet with a team to work on a project is, 'Here are the facts. Let's go.'" Dan works in a technical area, where Analyticals are often comfortable. He says, however, not only is it ineffective to build teams of entirely one Social Style, "It's boring."

To do his job more effectively, he realizes he sometimes must turn for help to team members with other Social Styles. "I'm very effective at pulling together all the necessary pieces for a project and breaking down all the options of what we need to do. I'm not as effective at getting other people fired up about what we have to do. So, it's helpful if I can find an Expressive, Amiable, or Driver to bounce ideas back and forth with me. They have skills I don't have, and I have skills they don't have, so we all contribute our strengths and find we want to get to the same end point."

Dan also taps team diversity in other ways. In team meetings to launch a new initiative, for example, Dan will kick things off, set the agenda, clarify the objectives, and explain the plan he wants to drive. "But if my point is not coming through, if people are not showing enthusiasm, I might toss the leadership of the meeting to one of our Expressives for a while to take a different tack."

SELLING IS EASIER WITH SOCIAL STYLES IN MIND

First of all, it's important to remember that everybody sells, not just salespeople. Whether we are selling real estate, our ideas, or ourselves, at times, we are all trying to move people to make decisions in our favor. For this purpose, understanding Social Styles is a potent tool.*

---

* If you sell products or services for a living, you might want to read *Versatile Selling: Adapting Your Style So Customers Say "Yes!"* – another book in the Wilson Learning Library available from Nova Vista Publishing.

Joyce Jappelle sometimes tells stories in her Social Styles work-shops about business she has lost because she failed to make cus-tomers comfortable. "I also talk about the successes" she says, "about times when I have won business even when my price was higher than my competitor's because the client felt they could work in a relaxed and comfortable manner with me.

At Bourne Leisure Limited, salespeople often sell their holiday deals or caravans and trailer homes to couples, says Ann Horner, a se-nior executive with the UK-based company. The risk in not using So-cial Styles concepts in these situations is that a salesperson may end up with half a sale, which really adds up to no sale.

"If salespeople are more comfortable with one person than the oth-er in a couple, they can end up spending their time talking to the wrong person. Using Social Styles concepts in these situations takes on a whole new level of meaning."

Dan Gordon says a large part of the work his group does in the Yoplait & Snacks Unlimited Research and Development area in Gener-al Mills has to do with new-product development. "One dynamic we have to deal with is the different types of people involved in launching products. There are marketing folks, consumer insight specialists, en-gineering support people, the operations people who run the plants. We have to interact with all of them to sell our ideas.

"Social Styles helps me think about how to relate with the various styles of people within each of those groups differently. In one case I was working with a Driver marketing director about plans to intro-duce a new product. I was in my analytical mode, providing data and consumer information about why we should go ahead. I sensed she wasn't listening. She wanted to cancel the project and was citing other consumer information that I thought was inaccurate. I finally realized we were both too much into our own modes and I needed to step back and take a different approach."

The advantage to having had his own team go through Social Styles training, Dan says, is that they have a common language for dealing with these kinds of challenges. "We can use it to break down barriers. We agree it's fine to be in any Social Style quadrant, but we also all have to learn to be versatile. Social Styles can be a great tension breaker when we're interacting or selling to each other."

Joyce Jappelle sums it all up quite succinctly: "Honestly, when I use Social Styles, I'm better at what I do, and things are easier for me and for the people I'm working with. When I don't use it, things get harder."

RECOGNIZE WHEN YOU ARE THE ONE IN BACK-UP

Back-Up happens. Stress mounts and relationships become tense and tenuous. When you are looking at relationships that are in trouble, it's important to first ask yourself, "What can I do to resolve this issue? How can I help the other person feel more comfortable so we can find a resolution that is mutually beneficial? Is this coming from my side or theirs, or maybe from both of us?"

In the heat of a difficult interaction, it's not uncommon to have everything you know about Social Styles disappear into a dark recess of your brain, warns Joyce Jappelle – even for people who have been using the tool for years.

Case in point: "I was visiting my Mom, who is 85, and I was trying to help her work out a problem with her long distance phone service," Joyce says. "I was trying to get her a credit on her account. When I called the phone company I got bounced around from department to department, and eventually ended up talking a second time to the person I first started with. I was so frustrated that when she got back on the line I asked, sarcastically, 'How could a phone company not know how to transfer a call?'

"I finally got transferred to the right person – a woman named Tiffany – who said she would stay with me and get me through the situation. But I started out asking, 'Why should I think you can help me after all the times I've already been transferred?' She said she understood I was upset and, although she was going to transfer me back to the first department again, she would stay on the line and explain everything so I wouldn't have to go through it all again.

"Suddenly I recognized that I was in Back-Up. I wasn't feeling very good about how I had behaved, so I apologized and told Tiffany she used good skills in diffusing my anger. She laughed and said, 'I knew you were upset and figured that's what it would take to deal the situation to your satisfaction. Compared to some of the calls we get, you weren't bad at all.'"

The reminder from Joyce is that relationships can be pleasant or painful, and Social Styles concepts offer the chance to do things "the better way," If we are aware of our own roles, influences, and reactions we can ensure that things go well. When things become unpleasant, we could be in Back-Up and need to use Social Styles skills to get an interaction back to the point where a relationship can be productive.

James Miller remembers going through a tough Back-Up situation with a boss. "She was an Expressive. But we were going through some tough times and being pushed on some deployment schedules. This was one of the nicest people I've ever known, but I saw some dramatic changes in her behaviors. She began attacking, quite viciously. It bothered me so much that I got out the old materials from my Social Styles workshop and refreshed myself on Back-Up Behavior. I immediately felt better knowing this was a predictable behavior for her style, since the first Back-Up Behavior for Expressives is Attacking. This is what happens when you put people under excessive stress. Underneath, I believed she was still the caring leader I had always known."

One of the breakthroughs for Tevilla Riddell in applying her knowledge of Social Styles was recognizing that, whether things are going well or not so well, "It isn't about people liking or disliking me, it's just that they may have different needs in terms of communication styles."

Bob Davis advises, "Withhold judgment. Prior to Social Styles training, I would often judge people with different styles as difficult, obnoxious, not caring, or worse. Now I recognize that often others are not doing anything to me, they are simply being who they are with no ill intent or desire to make me crazy. The way they behave is simply how they landed on the planet."

DON'T EXPECT RECIPROCITY

"One of the biggest mistakes I've ever made with Social Styles is thinking that just because I exhibited Versatility with someone else that it would always be reciprocated – that they would be versatile with me in response," says Bob Davis. "My experience is that more often than not, Versatility *does* breed Versatility. . . But let's be realistic; occasionally in life there are jerks."

The best strategy for thinking about reciprocity is to plan for little and relish whatever you get.

CONSISTENCY AND INTEGRITY MATTER MOST

Ultimately, evaluating your own Social Style and modifying your behavior to increase your Versatility is based on understanding how other people see you. Unless you walk around with a mirror in front of you all day, you are really not able to observe your own behavior, no matter how high your level of self-awareness. And, even if you could watch your every interaction, you might be as surprised by what you see, as most people are when they hear their own voice tape recorded. We all have a strong tendency to say, "That's not me." That's why it can be difficult to assess your own Social Style.

Perhaps the most important advice we can give you is to remember to be true to who you are, wherever you land in the Social Style matrix. Making simple, consistent modifications in your behaviors over time is the best formula for ensuring trust, confidence, and comfort with the important people in your life. If you say one thing and do another, or radically change the way you communicate with people from one day to the next, they won't know what to believe. That kind of inconsistency violates what people expect, and is certain to cause discomfort.

"If I could offer only one piece of advice to a new user of Social Styles," says Ann Horner, "I would say *really* believe when you hear people say there is no best place on the Social Style matrix. Know that all styles are valuable. Yes, it's probably true that in some companies you have to be a certain style to achieve the highest roles, but it most places there is not a specific style required for a specific role. In Bourne Leisure, we see every style at every level."

Hans Fenner of Capita-Consulting echoes that advice. "All the influencing strategies of the four different Social Styles can be successful, and all of them can fail. To influence others successfully, we have to accept that all humans negotiate and relate on the basis of only their own perceptions. And we have to become sensitive about how our own style is perceived by the people we want to influence."

DON'T TRY TO BE SOMEONE ELSE

There is a quote we like from poet and writer Maya Angelou:

> *"I note the obvious differences in the human family. Some of us are serious, some thrive on comedy. I note the obvious differences between each sort and type, but we are more alike, my friends, than we are unalike."*

We share her words as one last reminder before you begin your full-fledged efforts to use the Social Styles tools you have learned. We all tend to think our own Social Style is the best. Some people think the safest strategy is to find a way to force changes in our style so we land somewhere in the middle of the matrix. Neither is true.

The four Social Styles aren't better or worse, just different. We are all different, and yet we are the same in many ways. Whatever your Social Style, learning to modify your behaviors in response to those similarities and differences, while staying true to who you are, will have a profound influence on your ability to build successful relationships with Analyticals, Drivers, Amiables and Expressives. *And that's everybody.*

HOW TO ADAPT YOUR BEHAVIOR FOR ASK-, TELL-, TASK-, AND PEOPLE-DIRECTED STYLES

HOW TO BE MORE TASK-DIRECTED –
WITH ANALYTICALS AND DRIVERS

Be prepared; document things — Know your facts and have them in writing in case they are needed. Confirm understandings in writing and follow up if you need more information.

Be focused and factual; use PPP statements — Stick to business. Use Purpose, Process and Payoff statements to focus; avoid emotional appeals.

Mind the time — Begin and end on time; use a relatively formal, crisp style until you know what's expected of you.

State your opinions as questions — Give opinions in question form: "Do you think it would work if X?" or "We could try X. What do you think?"

HOW TO BE MORE ASK-DIRECTED –
WITH AMIABLES AND ANALYTICALS

Don't rush things — Allow them to get a feel for the situation, develop trust, assimilate information, and build confidence that their decisions won't be misjudged or too risky.

Take responsibility — Make it clear that you'll see things through so they will achieve their goals. If time and money issues aren't brought out, bring them up so everything is clear.

Provide assurances — Refer to other cases where you've succeeded, be clear about risks and alternatives, and make assurances.

Listen responsively — Since these people naturally ask rather than tell, you must draw them out.

People are either ask- or tell-assertive in the way they influence others, and either task- or people-directed in response to getting things done. You can adapt your behavior to these styles with these simple, practical ideas.

HOW TO BE MORE TELL-DIRECTED –
WITH DRIVERS AND EXPRESSIVES

Get to the point   Simplify and clarify your opinions. Don't be vague or ambiguous in an effort to be tactful. Say what you mean. Be clear where you stand.

Volunteer information   Don't wait for others to take the lead. Express your opinions.

Be willing to disagree   It's okay to disagree, as long as you do it without getting defensive or letting the challenge become personal.

Act on your convictions   Take a stand. Make decisions quickly.

Initiate conversation   Take the lead on introducing ideas and solutions.

HOW TO BE MORE PEOPLE-DIRECTED –
WITH AMIABLES AND EXPRESSIVES

Verbalize your feelings   Talk openly about how you feel about the issues. You can establish better relationships by acknowledging your honest reactions.

Pay personal compliments Sincere, legitimate compliments are always welcome. Don't hesitate to state positive sentiments, or to find indirect ways to say good things about the person.

Be willing to spend time Pay attention to feelings. You may not see a connection
on personal relationships between personal involvement and achieving goals, but friendship and sensitivity can build loyalty.

Make small talk; socialize Stay focused on your goals and objectives, but also talk about non-business topics.

Social Style Summary

Use this chart to refresh yourself on Social Syles from time to time. If you do so repeatedly, a great deal of the content will become habitual for you and your Versatility will steadily improve.

	ANALYTICAL	AMIABLE	DRIVER	EXPRESSIVE
PRIMARY ASSET	Systematic	Supportive	Focused	Energizing
BACK-UP BEHAVIOR	Avoid	Acquiesce	Autocratic	Attack
FOR GROWTH NEEDS TO	Decide	Initiate	Listen	Check
STRONGEST PERSONAL MOTIVATOR	Respect	Approval	Results	Recognition
NEEDS CLIMATE THAT	Describes	Supports	Commits	Collaborates
LET THEM SAVE	Face	Relationships	Time	Effort
MAKE EFFORT TO BE	Accurate	Agreeable	Efficient	Stimulating
SUPPORT THEIR	Principles and thinking	Relationships and feelings	Conclusions and actions	Visions and intuitions
STRESS BENE-FITS THAT ANSWER	HOW problem is solved	WHY solution is best	WHAT solution will do	WHO else has used
FOR DECISIONS GIVE THEM	Data and evidence	Assurances and guarantees	Options and probabilities	Testimony and incentives
FOLLOW UP WITH	Service	Support	Action	Attention

Resources

IF YOU WOULD LIKE TO LEARN MORE ABOUT SOCIAL STYLE SKILLS

The best way to learn Social Styles and Versatility skills is to take one of Wilson Learning's Social Styles workshops, "Building Relationship Versatility" or "Managing Interpersonal Relationships." You will learn about your own style, get practice in recognizing others', become more versatile, recognize Back-Up Behavior in action, and learn how to reduce tension with people of each style.

You'll also get a personal profile with objective feedback on your real Social Style. Many programs on personality types assume that people can recognize their own style, but nearly 40 years of Wilson Learning research proves this wrong. Most people benefit greatly from their personalized report, which consolidates others' observations about your Social Style and level of Versatility. Social Styles workshops are available in more than 20 culturally adapted, translated versions worldwide. To learn more, visit www.wilsonlearning.com.

"Social Styles has been a real boon to me. After 20 years of extensive training in many different areas, it is the most effective training I've ever received. And I have colleagues who feel the same way."

James Miller, Manager of Software Development, Qwest

"I'm not sure I can quantify the value of using Social Styles, but I know I would not want to do my job without it."

Ann Horner, Main Board Director, Bourne Leisure Limited

The Social Styles Handbook, Revised Edition (ISBN 978-90-77256-33-6)
192 pages, softcover, with models, charts, anecdotes, index and resource lists.
US$19.95, €19.95

IF YOU'D LIKE TO LEARN MORE ABOUT VERSATILE SELLING SKILLS

Managing Interpersonal Relations, the program that pioneered Versatility techniques, was developed by Wilson Learning in the early 1970s. Ongoing refinement has led to the current program, *The Versatile Salesperson*. With more than a million graduates worldwide, Versatility is a proven asset to any sales process.

The Versatile Salesperson is available for both classroom and e-learning environments. A suite of tools supports ongoing learning with specialized planning checklists, advisory guidelines, a manager's tool kit, a CD-ROM reinforcement program, and other resources. A specially adapted version for the pharmaceutical industry, *The Versatile Pharmaceutical Representative*, is also available.

The program is used by organizations of all sizes and in a wide range of business and non-profit sectors. Culturally adapted translations are available in 19 dialects and languages. In addition to the pharmaceutical industry program, custom versions for salespeople and sales managers in the health care, retail, travel and leisure, automotive, high tech, IT, manufacturing, financial, insurance, capital equipment and other industries are also available. Find out more about *The Versatile Salesperson* and Wilson Learning locations by visiting www.wilsonlearning.com.

"If there is one factor that differentiates high performing salespeople, it is Versatility – the ability to adapt one's approach and style of communication to meet the personal needs and expectations of the customer. Every salesperson will acknowledge that their selling skills work better with some customers than with others. The skills in The Versatile Salesperson *help salespeople adapt to all types of customers and help ensure success."*

Ron Remillard, Director of the Sales Training and Development Institute, Georgia Pacific Corporation

"The concepts in Versatile Selling changed my career and my life. I've been through a lot of training, and even after 33 years in sales I try to keep learning. Social Styles, Versatility and the Wilson Learning approach to sales have given me the solid foundation I needed to achieve the success that I've had.

W. Jacques Gibbs, Investment Advisor

Versatile Selling (ISBN 978-90-77256-03-9, Revised Edition 978-90-77256-35-0)
160 pages, softcover, with models, charts, anecdotes, index and resource lists.
US$18.95, € 18.95

IF YOU'D LIKE TO LEARN MORE
ABOUT COUNSELOR SELLING SKILLS

Wilson Learning began offering Sales Sonics, the predecessor to *The Counselor Salesperson* program, in 1965. To date, more than a million participants around the world have learned the Counselor mindset and skills presented in this program, in both classroom and e-learning environments.

Organizations of all sizes and in a wide range of business and non-profit sectors use this program. Culturally adapted translations and custom versions for salespeople are available in 19 dialects and languages. Custom versions for salespeople and sales managers in the pharmaceutical, health care, retail, travel and leisure, automotive, high tech, IT, manufacturing, financial, insurance, capital equipment and other industries are also available. Find out more by visiting www.wilsonlearning.com.

"Wilson Learning played a critical role in the reinvention of our sales force and our clients' perception of our value."

Ron DeLio, Chief Operating Officer,
Strategic Travel Solutions Division, Rosenbluth International

"We've used the Counselor method for more than 20 years and have thousands of graduates of the course. Our mission is 'To be the best in the eyes of our customers, employees and shareholders,' which means 'Do what's right,' 'Do the best you can,' and 'Help customers, employees and shareholders get what they want.' The Counselor method has been and continues to be the CORE of our way of accomplishing our mission."

Ed Gilbertson, Manager, Sales & Management Training, TRANE,
An American Standard Company

"These Wilson Learning methods are 'how we do business.' They are what sets us apart from our competitors and the reason why our customers rate us more highly in customer satisfaction than our peers. In the Counselor method we have discovered the sales system solution that delivers on our customers' needs."

Paul Bryant, Senior Manager,
Financial Services, Suncorp Metway Ltd.

Win-Win Selling (ISBN Revised Edition 978-90-88720-01-7, Third Edition, 978-90-77256-34-3) 160 pages, softcover, with models, charts, anecdotes, index and resource lists. US$18.95, € 18.95

Contributors

ABOUT THE AUTHORS

Tom Kramlinger, Ph.D., was a Senior Design Consultant at Wilson Learning. During more than 30 years with the company, he designed programs in sales and sales management and researched and designed special applications for clients in the capital equipment, financial, automotive, transport, chemical, IT, insurance and telecommunication industries. He taught *The Counselor Salesperson* pilot program in Japan and collaborated on its cultural adaptation there. His passion was creating and communicating advanced solutions for Fortune 500 global clients that integrate Wilson Learning technologies.

Michael Leimbach, Ph.D., is Vice President, Global Research and Development at Wilson Learning. He and his Global R&D team have created the innovative performance improvement systems that make Wilson Learning a leader in human performance improvement. He has been helping organizations gain sales force effectiveness for over 20 years. Michael has been involved with updating and enhancing all of Wilson Learning's sales-effectiveness programs and created Wilson Learning's sales-effectiveness diagnostic capabilities. He has published numerous professional articles and has presented before a wide range of clients and professional organizations around the world.

Ed Tittel, B.A., M.A., is a Senior Performance Consultant for Wilson Learning Worldwide. Ed has over 20 years' experience in the human performance improvement industry and has co-authored several Wilson Learning brand and custom offerings. During his tenure at Wilson Learning, he has consulted with Fortune 100 organizations throughout the United States, Europe and Asia. Prior to his work at Wilson Learning, Ed was a developer and demonstrator for the National Diffusion Network within the United States Department of Education.

David Yesford is the Vice President, Product Marketing for Wilson Learning Worldwide. He has spent 17 years helping organizations develop an understanding of effective consultative sales strategies. David has been involved with creating, updating and customizing sales effectiveness systems and most recently has lead Wilson Learning's effort to launch blended sales effectiveness capabilities. David's primary interest is to ensure that a person's performance improves in ways he or she values and the organization needs.

ABOUT THE PROJECT DEVELOPMENT TEAM

Brian McDermott is a consultant, business writer and editor with extensive experience in the field, particularly in the area of training. **Karien Sticker** is a graphics designer specialized in instructional page design. **Wouter Geukens** is a graphics designer specializing in books. **Andrew Karre** is an editor and book designer.

All the authors at Wilson Learning and the Nova Vista Publishing staff wish to thank the team, and others who lent their expertise, for their enthusiasm, dedication and resourcefulness in developing this book.

Index

A

Adapting behavior, 19, 33, 50
  With Analyticals, 99-102
  With Drivers, 118-120
  With Amiables, 137–139
  With Expressives, 155–157

Amiables, 12, 14, 29, 31, 60, 125-146

Analyticals, 12, 14, 28-29, 31, 39, 60, 88-106

Assertiveness, 24-34, 46-47, 60, 67-68, 167

Assertiveness behaviors, 23-32, 67-68, 118, 157, 167

Assertiveness continuum, 25-26, 32, 67-68

B

Back-Up behavior, 59-68, 103, 120, 140, 157, 176-177, 182-183

Body language, 11, 25, 27-28, 56, 63, 74, 77, 81, 86-87, 90–91, 97, 110-111, 113, 127, 130, 132, 140, 147, 160, 167-168

C

Changing your Social Style, 20, 171

Comfort zone, 34, 43, 46-47, 50, 53

Commonality, 74, 83, 90, 95, 114, 134, 152, 169

Competence, 74, 83, 95, 109, 114, 133, 135, 149, 152, 167

Corballis, Michael, 10

Correctness, 22, 130

Credibility, 4, 19, 71, 73, 83, 92-93, 95, 100, 114, 133, 135, 149, 151-152, 158, 161

D

Davis, Bob, 163-164, 177-178

Drivers, 12, 14, 29, 31, 60, 107–124

E

Entry, 71

Expressives, 12, 14, 29, 31, 58, 61, 145-163

F

Feeling, 54-58 see also Thinking

Fenner, Hans, 164, 179

Fight or flight Back-Up behavior, 59-68, 103, 121, 141, 157, 161

First meetings, 9-14, 17, 71-73, 167-170, 172-174

G

Gordon, Dan, 172, 175

H
Habit, 17, 48-53, 56
Horner, Ann, 44, 51, 56, 89, 175, 179

I
Identifying Social Styles, 20, 23, 50–54
Intervene with ask-directed person in flight mode, 62, 65-68, 103, 141

J
Jappelle, Joyce, 34, 141, 168, 175-176
Judgment, 28, 55, 65, 163, 173, 177

K
Kramlinger, Tom, 169, 172, 186

L
Language, 10, 21, 25, 56, 63, 77, 81, 90, 97, 130, 132, 140, 160, 167, 171, 175
Leadership, 45, 56, 76, 80, 102, 139, 174, 191
Leimbach, Michael, 186
Listen, Share, Clarify, Problem-solve, Ask for Action, see LSC-PA
LSCPA, 62, 64-69, 103, 121, 141, 158
   Listen, 62-63, 77, 82, 151, 158, 160-161, 167
   Share, 61-63, 65, 74, 158-159, 169
   Clarify, 62-63, 65, 67-68, 79, 81, 94-95, 98, 115, 124, 174, 181
   Problem-Solve, 62, 64
   Ask for Action, 62, 64
Luce, Don, 166

M
Mehrabian, Albert, 10
Miller, James, 19, 23, 104, 122, 164, 170-171, 177, 183
Misperceptions about specific Social Styles
   Amiables, 127, 142
   Analyticals, 91, 105
   Drivers, 110, 122
   Expressives, 147, 159

N
Neutralize tell-directed person in fight mode, 62, 65, 67-68, 121, 157, 161
Nonverbal communication, 11, 25, 27-28, 56, 63, 74, 77, 81, 86-87, 90-91, 97, 110-111, 113, 127, 130, 132, 140, 147, 160, 167-168

O
O'Brien, Derek, 170

P
Pace, 93, 95-96, 113, 115, 124, 127, 129, 131-132, 139, 144, 160
People-directed responsiveness,

29, 52, 140
Platinum Rule, 171
Purpose, Process, Payoff (PPP),
  72, 94

Q
Questioning skills, 161
Questions, categories of, 75
  Best-least, 76, 83, 96, 150
  Fact-finding, 75-76, 83, 96, 115,
  150
  Feeling-finding, 76, 83, 96, 150
  Magic-wand, 76, 83, 97, 150
  Permission, 75, 83, 96, 150

R
References, 11, 98, 135, 148
Relationship tension, 36-41, 43,
  59-61, 70-71, 79, 83, 90, 99, 101,
  103, 106, 120, 129, 138
Research in Wilson Learning's
  Social Styles data base, 8,
  10-13, 24-26, 51
Responsiveness continuum, 27,
  32
Responsiveness, 24-34, 46-47, 52,
  167, 169
Riddell, Tevilla, 18, 43, 165, 177

S
Schoolcraft, Sherry, 21, 89, 158,
  171
Selling, 12, 174, 176, 184
Smith, Marilyn, 107, 158, 166
Social Styles Matrix, 29, 32, 109,

111, 163, 165-166
Social Styles Self-Profiler, 84–87
Stereotypes, 55, 165

T
Task tension, 3-4, 36-41, 60, 70-71
Task-directed responsiveness, 27,
  29
Tell-directed assertiveness, 25,
  29, 52
Tension, 18, 23, 36-41, 43, 59-61,
  63, 70-71, 79, 83, 176. *See also*
  relationship tension and task
  tension
  Rising and falling, 38, 77
Thinking, 56–58. See also feeling
Tittel, Ed, 186
Trust, 13, 19, 22, 30, 37, 42-47, 71,
  74, 78-79, 81

U
Understanding, 18-19, 50, 55, 58,
  74-75, 81

V
Verbal and nonverbal behavior,
  11, 25, 27, 74, 91
Versatility, 8, 12, 14, 34–35, 38,
  42-43, 47, 51, 53, 73, 77, 81

W
Wilson, Larry, 3, 7, 171, 191

Y
Yesford, David, 187

OTHER TITLES IN THE WILSON LEARNING LIBRARY

Win-Win Selling: Turning Customer NEEDS into SALES.
Differentiating your company's products and services is a big chal-lenge today. But a company's sales force can become a significant differentiator, and gain sustainable advantages, if it adopts the Counselor approach. A win-win mind and skill set, based on trust, problem-solving and side-by-side work between seller and customer, makes buying easy. And because the seller stays by the customer after the sale, the door opens for long-term, expanding business.

Fortune 500 global and other companies in 30 countries have used Wilson Learning's Counselor approach for years with astonishing success. The book gives the million-plus people who have taken Wil-son Learning's *The Counselor Salesperson* course a refresher, and gives others a powerful sales process. Larry Wilson, author of *One Minute Salesperson* and founder of Wilson Learning (1965) wrote the foreword to the book. It's indispensable for salespeople and sales managers, who say it's solid, practical and really works.

"The Counselor Approach enhanced our leadership position by helping our sales and marketing organization dis-cover what is most important in our marketplace. As a result, we are adding more value to our customers as a means of advocating for the patient."

Dan Schlewitz, Vice President Sales,
Medtronic CRM

Win-Win Selling (ISBN Revised Edition 978-90-88720-01-7, Third Edition 978-90-77256-34-3)
160 pages, 160 X 230 cm (6" x 9")
Suggested retail price: € 18.95, US$18.95
Models, charts, anecdotes, an index and other resources.

Versatile Selling: Selling the Way Your Customer Wants to Buy.
This book presents the concepts and tools of *The Social Styles Hand-book*, specifically adapted for the needs of salespeople. The powerful yet simple skill of Versatility – the ability to read and adapt to the natural behavior of your customers – makes them feel comfortable and ready to buy, and has been proven to increase sales measurably. Learn to assess your own Social Style (Driver, Analytical, Amiable, or Expressive) and the style of your customer. That way you know how your customer wants to be treated, and you can adapt your own behavior to the customer's specific needs and expectations. You will also know how to respond to and decrease unproductive tension and get back to productive collaboration, because you know how to handle Back-Up Behaviors of customers of different styles. No matter what sales process you use, this book will help you work better with every customer.

"The concepts in Versatile Selling changed my career and my life. I've been through a lot of training, and even after 33 years in sales I try to keep learning. Social Styles, Versatility and the Wilson Learning approach to sales have given me the solid foundation I needed to achieve the success I've had."

W. Jacques Gibbs, Investment Advisor

Versatile Selling (ISBN 978-90-77256-03-9, Revised Edition 978-90-77256-35-0)
160 pages, 160 X 230 cm (6" x 9")
Suggested retail price: € 18.95, US$18.95
Models, charts, anecdotes, an index and other resources.

CAREERS

I Just Love My Job!
Roy Calvert, Brian Durkin, Eugenio Grandi and Kevin Martin, in the Quarto Consulting Library (ISBN 978-90-77256-02-2, softcover, 192 pages, $19.95)

Taking Charge of Your Career
Leigh Bailey (ISBN 978-90-77256-13-8, softcover, 96 pages, $14.95)

LEADERSHIP AND INNOVATION

Grown-Up Leadership
Leigh Bailey and Maureen Bailey (ISBN 978-90-77256-09-1, softcover, 144 pages, $18.95)

Grown-Up Leadership Workbook
Leigh Bailey (ISBN 978-90-77256-15-2, softcover, 96 pages, $14.95)

Leading Innovation
Brian McDermott and Gerry Sexton (ISBN 978-90-77256-05-3, softcover, 160 pages, $18.95)

Time Out for Leaders
Donald Luce and Brian McDermott (ISBN 978-90-77256-10-7, hardcover with marker ribbon, $19.95; ISBN 978-90-77256-30-5, softcover, $14.95)

SALES

Time Out for Salespeople
Nova Vista Publishing's Best Practices Editors (ISBN 978-90-77256-14-5, hardcover with marker ribbon, 272 pages, $19.95; ISBN 978-90-77256-31-2, softcover, 272 pages, $14.95)

Get-Real Selling, Revised Edition
Michael Boland and Keith Hawk (ISBN 978-90-77256-32-9, softcover, 144 pages, $18.95)

CUSTOMER SERVICE AND ORGANIZATIONAL TRANSFORMATION

Service Excellence @ Novell
Nova Vista Publishing's Best Practices Editors (ISBN 978-90-77256-11-4, softcover, 112 pages, $18.95)

SCIENCE PARKS, ECONOMICS, ECOLOGY OF INNOVATION

What Makes Silicon Valley Tick?
Tapan Munroe, Ph.D., with Mark Westwind, MPA (ISBN 978-90-77256-28-2, softcover, 192 pages, $19.95)

You can read about Wilson Learning Library titles on pages 183-85 and 191.

Visit **www.novavistapub.com** for sample chapters, reviews, links and ordering.